Please return / renew by date shown.
You can renew at: **norlink.norfolk.gov.uk**
or by telephone: **0344 800 8006**
Please have your library card & PIN ready.

2 1 SEP 2013

NORFOLK LIBRARY
AND INFORMATION SERVICE

D1353226

 Longman

 York Press

The poem by W.H Auden on p. 106 is quoted by permission of Faber & Faber

Robin Sowerby is hereby identified as author of this work in accordance with
Section 77 of the Copyright, Designs and Patents Act 1988

YORK PRESS
322 Old Brompton Road, London SW5 9JH

PEARSON EDUCATION LIMITED
Edinburgh Gate, Harlow,
Essex CM20 2JE, United Kingdom
Associated companies, branches and representatives throughout the world

First published 2001
15 14 13 12 11 10

ISBN: 978-0-582-43154-6

Designed by Vicki Pacey
Phototypeset by Gem Graphics, Trenance, Mawgan Porth, Cornwall
Colour reproduction and film output by Spectrum Colour
Produced by Pearson Education Asia Limited, Hong Kong
(EPC)

Contents

PART ONE

INTRODUCTION

HOW TO STUDY AN EPIC NARRATIVE POEM (IN PROSE TRANSLATION)

Studying a long narrative poem on your own requires self-discipline and a carefully thought-out work plan in order to be effective.

- You will need to read the work more than once. Start by reading it quickly for pleasure, then read it slowly and thoroughly.
- On your second reading make detailed notes on the plot, characters and themes. Further readings will generate new ideas.
- Make sure you understand all the mythological references. Look names up in a dictionary if necessary.
- Remember that, though you are reading it in modern prose, the work is from a different culture and time. Make an imaginative effort to read it on its own terms, noting how it differs from modern stories set in the modern world.
- **Epic** poems feature epic heroes. What are the characteristics of heroic behaviour in this work and how do they differ from those exhibited by other heroic figures?
- Think about the way in which the narrative unfolds: the time-scheme and the different settings may be a key to its structure and organisation.
- Are words, images or motifs repeated so as to give the work a pattern? Do such patterns help you to understand the work's themes?
- It is difficult when commenting on a work in translation to make precise points about its style. But think of its style in broad terms, noting such features as the recurring **epithets**, the extended **similes**, the set speeches, the intervention of the divine. Compare with another translation if you can.
- Does the work present a moral and just world?
- Cite exact sources for all quotations. Wherever possible find your own examples from the work to back up your own opinions.
- Always express your ideas in your own words.

This York Note offers an introduction to the *Aeneid* and cannot substitute for close reading of the text and the study of secondary sources.

Virgil's *Aeneid*, coming after Homer's *Iliad* and *Odyssey*, is the third of the great **epics** from the Graeco-Roman world, and completes the Trojan saga by taking it in a new direction. For the Trojan Aeneas, at the behest of the gods, undertakes an epic journey and a grand task in leading the remnant of his people to a new destiny overseas, to Italy where their descendants will found the city of Rome. Aeneas's account of the fall of Troy brought about by the stratagem of the Wooden Horse, his encounter with the Carthaginian queen Dido, and his visit to the underworld to meet the spirit of his dead father Anchises are among the most celebrated narratives in world literature. In these encounters, Aeneas takes a rather passive role but this is a consequence of the larger part that he is to play in the grand scheme of things envisaged in the poem, as T.S. Eliot recounts in his essay 'What is a Classic?':

> Aeneas is himself, from first to last, a 'man in fate', a man who is neither an adventurer nor a schemer, neither a vagabond nor a careerist, a man fulfilling his destiny, not under compulsion or arbitrary decree, and certainly from no stimulus to glory, but by surrendering his will to a higher power behind the gods who would thwart or direct him. ... he is not, in a human sense, a happy or successful man. But he is the **symbol** of Rome; and as Aeneas is to Rome, so is ancient Rome to Europe. Thus Virgil acquires the centrality of the unique classic; he is at the centre of European civilisation; in a position which no other poet can share or usurp. The Roman Empire and the Latin language were not any old empire and language but an empire and a language with a unique destiny in relation to ourselves; and the poet in whom that Empire and language came to consciousness and expression is a poet of unique destiny.

In Eliot's view, and he has principally in mind the Virgil who composed the *Aeneid*, Virgil is 'our classic, the classic of all Europe'. Whether this is a claim we wish to accept, we can see why Eliot made it and it could scarcely be made convincingly about any other poem.

In Roman times the *Aeneid* was soon regarded as a classic, and since antiquity, wherever Latin has been known, Virgil's poetry has been read with admiration. He has been admired chiefly on three accounts: as a master of the Latin language, as the voice of Roman civilisation, and as a poet who expresses a sympathy for human suffering that gives his poetry a universal significance transcending Rome.

Virgil has been regarded in later time as the great example of the patriotic poet who in his *Aeneid* celebrates his city's glories and sings Augustus Caesar's praises. In the speech of Anchises in which the Roman destiny to rule and impose peace is revealed to Aeneas, Rome herself rejoices in her offspring, as Cybele, the great mother of the gods, rejoices in her mighty Olympian progeny (Book 6, lines 781–7). Strategically placed after the passage on Romulus, Rome's first founder, comes the praise of Augustus Caesar who is to restore the Golden Age of peace and virtue to Italy and extend Roman power to the utmost limits. He is likened to the civilising hero Hercules and to the god Bacchus, the law-giver and bringer of peace (lines 789–805). Rome and her great men are likened to gods and heroes, just as the gods themselves are associated with Roman values when, for example, Neptune calms the seas as a grave Roman orator might calm the mob (Book 1, lines 148–56), or when Vulcan diligently sets about his task like a dutiful Roman matron who sacrifices herself to work for her children (Book 8, lines 407–15). It is not therefore surprising that the *Aeneid* has been regarded as the epic of Rome; indeed in the prophecy of Jupiter the whole of human history is seen to be working towards the Augustan peace (Book 1, lines 257–96).

Virgil's praise of Caesar as the man of destiny in whom the Roman achievement is to be fully realised has led critics to a thorough-going political interpretation of the *Aeneid*. In the preface to his translation of 1697, John Dryden (1631–1700) expresses the belief that Virgil wrote the poem to recommend the rule of Augustus to his contemporaries, and he considers that in the character and actions of Aeneas the character and career of Augustus are prefigured. Quite apart from the three prophetic passages which refer directly to the Roman future (Jupiter's prophecy, the speech of Anchises in Hades, and the description of the shield of Aeneas), there are what may seem to be allusions to contemporary history in the present action of the *Aeneid*. For example, Aeneas promises to build a temple dedicated to Apollo (Book 6, lines 69–70), and this Augustus did in 28BC. Clearly none of Virgil's contemporaries could have read the Dido and Aeneas episode without thinking of the recent history of Antony and Cleopatra (see Background) and seeing Aeneas as a character who, unlike Antony, behaves like a true Roman and leaves.

But if Virgil's design was what Dryden thought it to have been, why did he choose to develop the Dido episode in the way that he did? Most admirers of Virgil have agreed that this is the most intense part of the poem. If this is so, is it not odd that Virgil's creative powers should have been most fully released in an **episode** in which the hero of his poem is deliberately seen in a poor light, which risks alienating the reader from Aeneas and all that he is supposed to stand for? Virgil could have represented Dido as an irresistibly sensual figure like Shakespeare's Cleopatra, or as a sorceress like Medea who uses potions and spells in her love affair with Jason, or as a figure like Homer's Calypso who tries to beguile and constrain Odysseus against his real will. But Virgil's Dido is like none of these: she is sympathetically represented, and in leaving her Aeneas comes away, humanly speaking, with little credit. Considering this episode in the light of his interpretation, Dryden concluded that Virgil had made a mistake. Similarly **Romantic** critics have argued that Virgil lost control of his imagination in Book 4. But will this do? Is the relation between the poem and history and between Aeneas and Augustus as clear-cut and straightforward as Dryden would have us believe? Might not Virgil be deliberately making a point about the cost of the Roman destiny to those who stand in its way?

In fact it can be argued that the *Aeneid* is a great poem, not simply because it raises admiration for the Roman achievement (or, in a less admiring view, gives expression to the Roman will to power), but because it dramatises the cost of the Roman achievement. This applies not only to those who found themselves on a collision course with Roman destiny, but also to the victors themselves, for Aeneas appears to be as much a sacrificial victim as Dido or the Italians whom he defeats. It can be said that his main virtue *pietas*, 'duty', involves constant self-sacrifice. It is the cost of it all that exercises Virgil's imagination: *tantae molis erat Romanam condere gentem*, 'So heavy was the cost of founding the Roman race' (Book 1, line 33). There is no happy or easy affirmation of the will to civilisation in the *Aeneid*; Virgil knew all about civilisation and its discontents. (This is further explored in Critical Approaches.)

In a poem that has been so widely read over such a long period, there will naturally be dissident voices and reservations expressed. In an essay 'On the Modern Element in Literature', Matthew Arnold (1822–88) while admiring Virgil nevertheless was prepared to question his poem's greatness:

> Does he represent the epoch in which he lived, the mighty Roman world of his time, as the great poets of the great epoch of Greek life represented theirs, in all its fulness, in all its significance?

Another reservation was expressed by T.S. Eliot in his essay 'Virgil and the Christian World':

> There is tenderness and **pathos** enough in the *Aeneid*. But love is never given, to my mind, the significance that *pietas* is given. … If we are not chilled, we at least feel ourselves, with Virgil, to be moving in a kind of emotional twilight.

Eliot admires Virgil's delicate sensibility, and most readers respond to Virgilian pity for mankind suffering under a variety of horrors both physical and psychological, and both natural and supernatural. But, he asks, does Virgil give us the full response to life that we find, for example, in Homer or Shakespeare?

PART TWO

Summaries & Commentaries

There have been hundreds of editions of Virgil's Aeneid *since the first printing of the text in the late fifteenth century. An authoritative text is to be found in* Virgil: Opera, *edited by R.A.B. Mynors, Oxford Classical Texts, Clarendon Press, Oxford, 1969.*

In the preparation of this Note intended primarily for students reading a translation, the following version has been used: Virgil: The Aeneid: A New Prose Translation *by David West, Penguin, Harmondsworth, 1990 and reprinted subsequently. This edition has the line numbers of the Latin printed at the side of the text. Quotations in this Note are all from the above edition, while line numbers refer to line numbers in the original Latin so that it should be possible to use this Note with any reasonably literal version or with any version where the lines of the original Latin are indicated.*

Latin names are given the form in which they appear in the Penguin version. In the case of mythological figures who have both a Greek and a Roman name, as a general rule the Roman form is used except when the context is specifically Greek. For example Ulysses and Jupiter are given their Greek names Odysseus and Zeus when reference is being made to them as they occur in the Homeric poems. Most of the place names mentioned can be found on The Map Showing the Voyage of Aeneas, which is therefore both historical and mythological.

Synopsis

The general design of the *Aeneid* is apparent in the opening lines. It is a poem of martial exploits whose hero Aeneas, a homeless exile after the Greeks have destroyed his native Troy, is compelled to undertake a perilous journey of **epic** proportions, leading the remnants of his people from their old imperial city of Troy to a new destiny in Italy. Aeneas's destiny is not a matter of his own choice and will, it is imposed upon him by the gods and entails hardship and sacrifice. At the outset Virgil emphasises both the obstacles that must be overcome on the journey by land and sea (the subject of Books 1 to 6) and the suffering to be endured in the war in Italy before peace is established (the subjects of Books 7 to 12). For Aeneas's destiny, although divinely supported, is also divinely opposed, principally by the goddess Juno whose hatred of the Trojan race sets the poem in motion and continues throughout. Nevertheless, Aeneas endures all perils and dangers to found a city in which he and his followers can practise the religion they have brought with them from Troy. For Aeneas is not merely a warrior, he is the guardian of his nation's spiritual heritage which is to be perpetuated and transmitted to succeeding generations in Italy. His son will found Alba Longa and his descendant Romulus will found Rome. The climactic emphasis upon Rome at the end of the opening section suggests an historical concern beyond personal destiny. It is apparent from the start that Aeneas is caught between two worlds: a Trojan past and a Roman future.

The opening gives the broad context of past and future in which the present action is set, but the narrative starts *in medias res* (in the middle of things) seven years after the fall of Troy. In a storm raised by Juno the Trojans are shipwrecked on the African coast where they are offered shelter by the Carthaginian queen Dido (Book 1). While enjoying Dido's hospitality, Aeneas tells her of the sack of Troy (Book 2) and of his seven years' wandering from Troy (Book 3). After this retrospective narrative, there follows the ill-fated love affair of Dido and Aeneas (Book 4). Leaving Carthage, Aeneas sails to Sicily where he presides over funeral games on the anniversary of the death of his father Anchises (Book 5). From here he sails up the Italian coast to Cumae, and with the Sibyl as his guide descends into the underworld (where dwell the spirits of the dead) to be instructed in the future of his race by Anchises (Book 6). The Trojans then sail to the mouth of the Tiber, the site of the destined city to be named Lavinium, after Aeneas's future wife Lavinia, the daughter of Latinus, King of the Latins and ruler of Latium, the region of Italy in which the Trojans have landed. This marriage which will eventually confirm the union of Trojans and Latins is at first welcomed by Latinus, who, from earlier prophecies, recognises in Aeneas the stranger who is destined to be his son-in-law. However, Juno tries to prevent the match and provokes Turnus, prince of the neighbouring Rutulians and Lavinia's suitor, to oppose the incoming Trojans. Turnus rouses local opposition.

Fighting breaks out and both sides prepare for war (Book 7). Aeneas sails up the Tiber to seek allies and visits the site of Rome (Book 8). The remaining four books chart the course of the war in Latium, culminating in the death of Turnus at the hands of Aeneas in Book 12. As the epic began in the middle of things, so it ends abruptly without reference to Aeneas's marriage or the founding of Rome.

DETAILED COMMENTARIES

BOOK 1   The Trojans land at Carthage; Aeneas is received by Dido

Journeying to Italy the Trojans are shipwrecked on the African coast in a storm raised by Juno. Jupiter predicts a great destiny for Aeneas and his descendants. In disguise Venus tells Aeneas of his whereabouts and of the life story of Dido, the Carthaginian queen. She conveys him in a cloud to Carthage where he sees the friends he had thought lost, and is well received by Dido. At a banquet that evening, Dido by a trick of Venus begins to fall in love with Aeneas.

For comment on the poem's proposition, see the beginning of the Synopsis above.

The opposition of Juno who causes Aeolus to release the storm winds that drive the Trojans off course across the Mediterranean to North Africa is a constant theme amounting to a basic structural principle in the **epic**. The goddess is behind most of the actions that interfere with a smooth working out of the destiny that is to lead to the foundation of Rome. She also raises the opposition to the Trojans in Italy.

Like the Homeric Odysseus, Aeneas's first involvement in the poem is in a shipwreck, but unlike his Homeric counterpart Aeneas is not shown acting heroically: he is dejected by events and simply endeavours to cheer his men. He is involved in little heroic action in the first half of the poem.

The opening events lead swiftly by way of Venus's concern for her son Aeneas to Jupiter's speech prophesying the Roman empire and the *pax Augusta* which from his Olympian perspective is the grand climax of human history (lines 276–96). Virgil moves quickly to establish the broad historical dimension of his epic.

Accordingly Jupiter mollifies Carthaginian ferocity but our impression of the future enemies of Rome is hardly one of a people who have primitive passions that need to be restrained; on the contrary they are building a highly orderly and civilised society.

Our first glimpse of Carthage is through the eyes of Aeneas as he looks down from a nearby hill in wonder at the solid buildings rising where once there had been simple huts (lines 420–2). The Carthaginians are busily engaged not only in building but in choosing magistrates, making laws and establishing their senate (line 426). On one side a harbour is being excavated (line 427), for Carthage is to be a great trading power. Elsewhere the foundations of a theatre are being laid, for the city is not only to be grand but also cultivated (lines 427–9). In a poem that is ostensibly about the founding of Rome, Virgil here presents us with a deed of civilisation initiated not by Aeneas but, **ironically**, by Dido the founder of Rome's great rival and adversary. That Virgil wishes to raise our admiration for the disciplined energy of the Carthaginians is confirmed by the **simile** (lines 430–6) in which they are likened to bees in early summer, all busily engaged in the various tasks which are directed towards the making of honey fragrant with thyme. Implicit in the comparison is admiration both for the ordered purpose of the enterprise and for the beauty of the resulting product.

Virgil goes on to describe the temple of Juno in which Aeneas is to meet Dido. The grand temple has been built on a site where there had been discovered the head of a horse (line 444), deemed prophetic of Carthage's abundant resources and distinction in war. The temple is magnificent with much bronze (lines 447–9), but its art work with representations of Trojan sufferings (lines 456–93) expresses not the values of a war-like people but the Carthaginians' aesthetic sense and Dido's humanity; the Trojans are represented as suffering victims.

After their meeting, Dido prepares a sumptuous banquet with which to entertain her Trojan guests. There is much regal opulence, with a ceiling of panelled gold, purple coverlets, and silver and gold plate (lines 637–40). Amidst this magnificence the Carthaginians admire the beauty of the gifts that Aeneas bestows upon the bountiful Dido, gifts that are the relics of a civilisation comparably rich (lines 709–11). The dignified banquet and festivity conclude with wine and song, as the jewelled drinking bowl circulates and the bard Iopas sings to the accompaniment of his golden lyre of the sun and moon, of the creation of man and the animals and of the constellations and the seasons (lines 738–46). Carthage is therefore comparable in its magnificence, its opulence and its culture to Troy, and is a city where Aeneas might well be disposed to linger.

2 **the shores of Lavinium** named after Lavinia, daughter of Latinus, king of Latium, and future wife of Aeneas

4 **Juno** as the sister and wife of Jupiter, king of the gods, she is queen of heaven. She is the daughter of Saturn and is sometimes referred to as Saturnian Juno. She is a goddess of power and authority

7 **Alban fathers** Ascanius, Aeneas's son, moved from Lavinium and founded the city of Alba Longa near Mount Alba, not far from Rome (see lines 267–73)

12 **Tyre** later on (lines 330 ff.) Venus tells Aeneas how the Tyrians came from Tyre in Phoenicia (now the Lebanon) to Carthage in North Africa (now Tunisia)

16 **her armour** emblems of the goddess's power and authority. Juno was patroness of Carthage as, for example, Athene was patroness of Athens. She would naturally oppose a people whose descendants, according to the Fates, were to clash with the Carthaginians in a struggle for dominion over the Mediterranean in the Punic Wars

24 **Argos** a city in mainland Greece. The name was often used to indicate all Greece. Juno's hatred of the Trojans has roots in the past. She had supported the Greeks in the Trojan War

27 **the judgement of Paris** the second son of King Priam of Troy. Jupiter gave him the task of deciding which of the three senior goddesses was the fairest. Juno offered him wealth and power, Minerva offered renown in war and Venus offered him the most beautiful woman in the world, Helen, wife

of the Greek Menelaus, King of Sparta. Paris chose Venus and her gift. This not only offended Juno but caused the Trojan War. The Greeks sent an expedition to recover Helen after Paris had abducted her to Troy

28 **Dardanus** Dardanus, the founder of the Trojan race, was the product of one of Jupiter's illegitimate affairs

Ganymede a beautiful Trojan youth loved by Jupiter and carried off by him to Mount Olympus, where the gods dwell, to replace Hebe, Juno's daughter, as cupbearer to the gods

30 **Achilles** the ruthless chief warrior on the Greek side in the war against Troy

40 **Argives** Greeks from Argos. The Greeks are also sometimes called Danaans or Achaeans

41 **Ajax** on the night of Troy's fall Ajax had raped Cassandra, one of Priam's daughters, in the temple of Minerva. Later he boasted that he could get home without the help of the gods. Minerva borrowed her father Jupiter's thunderbolt

52 **Aeolus** a lesser god who owes his power and his place at the banquet table on Olympus to Juno. Nevertheless Juno offers him an inducement to gain his co-operation

97 **Diomede** in the fighting at Troy Aeneas was nearly killed by him but was rescued by his mother Venus (see *Iliad* Book 5, line 297)

99 **Hector** the death of Hector, the Trojans' strongest fighter, at the hands of Achilles is the climax of the *Iliad*

100 **Sarpedon** a son of Jupiter killed at Troy by the friend of Achilles, Patroclus (*Iliad*, Book 16)

Simois a river on the Trojan plain

113 **Lycians** a people who dwelt near Troy

125 **Neptune** when the Olympian gods came to power after replacing the Titans, Jupiter, Neptune and Pluto, all sons of Saturn, drew lots to divide the world between them. Neptune was allotted dominion over the sea, Jupiter ruled the sky and Pluto was king of the underworld. The **symbol** of Neptune's power is the trident, a spear with three prongs

144 **Triton and the sea nymph Cymothoe** lesser sea gods

200 **Scylla** a sea monster described at Book 3, lines 420–8

201 **Cyclopes** see Book 3, lines 655–83

223 **Jupiter** son of Saturn who created mankind and was the father of some of the gods. He is the most powerful of the Olympians, often referred to as their king, and his special province is the upper air where he controls

storms and clouds and sends rain (see Book 5, lines 693–9). His power is expressed in his thunderbolt. Another of his emblems is the eagle. The Romans built a temple to him on the highest of their seven hills, the Capitol, which overlooked their own legislative assembly, the Forum, and the whole region of Latium. He is associated with dominion and power (*imperium*) and with law and justice (*ius*). Hence his companion gods on the Capitol were Fides (Faithfulness or Fidelity) and Victoria (Victory).

229 **Venus** as mother of Aeneas, Venus petitions her father Jupiter on her son's behalf

235 **Teucer** son of Scamander, god of the river of the same name, which flowed by Troy. The Trojans, his descendants, are sometimes called Teucrians

242 **Antenor** a Trojan who after the fall of Troy sailed successfully round Greece to settle in Padua in North Italy

257 **Spare yourself these fears** as the source of all prophetic power it is fitting that he should declare what the fates intend for Aeneas and his descendants. After death Aeneas will be made a god

263 **a great war in Italy** in Italy Aeneas will not only establish outward defences for his community, its walls, but he will also fix laws, customs and institutions. The Latin word embracing all these is *mores*

268 **Ilium** another name for Troy, from Ilus, in some accounts the mythical founder of the city

282 **the toga** the civilian dress of the Romans; a kind of gown

284 **Assaracus** son of Tros (whence Trojans), grandfather of Aeneas's father Anchises

    Phthia the birthplace of Achilles

    Mycenae ruled by Agamemnon, leader of the Greek expedition to Troy. Like Argos Mycenae is sometimes used to represent Greece as a whole. Jupiter looks forward to the Roman conquest of Greece, completed in 146BC

286 **Caesar** not Julius Caesar but the emperor Augustus, who returned from his conquest of the Egyptian queen Cleopatra to a Roman triumph. When adopted by Julius Caesar, he became Caius Julius Caesar Octavianus. He took the name Augustus in 27BC. The name Julius is given to him here to mark the connection with Iulus. In 29BC Augustus dedicated a temple to Julius Caesar, and himself began to accept divine honours

292 **Vesta** Jupiter foresees a time of peace (the *pax Augusta*) and justice with the return of the old guardian gods of Rome. Vesta is the goddess of the

hearth and is associated with the essential spirit of the city (see Book 2, lines 296–7)

Quirinus the name given to Romulus, the first king of Rome, after he had become a divinity. Remus is the twin brother killed by Romulus. Their reconciliation in this passage **symbolises** the end to the civil discord, brought about by the regime of Augustus

294 **Gates of War** the gates of the temple of Janus: these were closed to mark a state of peace throughout the Roman state and were so closed by Augustus for only the third time in Roman history in 29BC (see Book 7, lines 601–17)

297 **Mercury** the messenger of the gods

329 **Diana sister of Apollo** she was the goddess of chastity and hunting

378 **the Penates** Aeneas carries actual images of the guardian gods of Troy. Every household has its resident gods, and so does the state which is a union of households. The Latin word is *penates* (see also Book 2, lines 293–4)

380 **my fatherland in Italy** Dardanus, the son of Jupiter, who married the daughter of Teucer and founded the city of Troy is said to have come originally from Italy. Aeneas is returning to the country of his race's origins. From Dardanus, the Trojans are sometimes called Dardans

381 **Phrygian** Phrygia is the area in which Troy was situated, now Turkey

415 **Paphos** a city in Cyprus where there was a particular cult of Venus. The fragrance of mysterious incense and the flowers at the altars of Venus are appropriate as she is the goddess of beauty. Aeneas recognises her by the beauty of her form and bearing

430 **like bees** to the ancients the social organisation of bees afforded an image of perfect order (see Virgil's fourth *Georgic*)

444 **the head of a spirited stallion** the horse, a symbol of war and wealth, appears on Carthaginian coins

458 **Achilles** his anger was directed not only against the Trojans, but against his own side, too, when the Greek leader Agamemnon, brother of Menelaus, deprived him of the slave girl allotted to him as a spoil of war (see *Iliad*, Book 1)

469 **Rhesus** a Thracian prince who came to help the Trojans. He was killed by Diomede and Ulysses on the first night of his landing. An oracle had told them that Troy would never be captured if the horses of Rhesus tasted the grass or water of Troy

464 **Troilus** one of Priam's younger sons and no match for the experienced warrior Achilles

479 **Pallas Athene** the loosened hair signifies grief. Pallas Athene is another name for Minerva, the goddess of war and wisdom. She, like Juno, was hostile to Troy as a result of the judgement of Paris. The robe would be draped over her statue

483 **Hector** in *Iliad*, Book 24 Homer tells how the aged Priam went at night to the tent of Achilles to ransom his son's body. Both gods and men disapproved of Achilles for his treatment of Hector's body but he dealt honourably with Priam

489 **Memnon** a son of the dawn, Aurora. He brought the Aethiopians to help the Trojans

491 **Penthesilea** Queen of the Amazons, warrior women, allies of the Trojans, who came from the Caucasus, an inhospitable region in central Asia. They sometimes cut off their right breasts so as to be free to use the bow

498 **Mount Cynthus** a mountain on the island of Delos (in the Aegean Sea) where Diana and her twin brother Apollo were born to Latona, mistress of Jupiter

499 **Diana** see note on line 329

547 **shades** spirits of the dead

569 **Saturn** a mythical king of Italy, later a god thought to be the father of Jupiter, to whom was ascribed the introduction of agriculture and the habits of civilised life in general. His reign was called the Golden Age (see Book 8, lines 319–27)

619 **the Greek Teucer** not to be confused with the Trojan Teucer referred to earlier; he was the brother of Ajax. His father expelled him from Salamis because he had not avenged the death of his brother who had committed suicide after being refused the arms of Achilles by the other Greek leaders. He founded a second Salamis in Cyprus with the help of Dido's father

658 **Cupid** the son of Venus. He has the form of a small boy, and is often represented as being blindfolded and carrying a bow and arrow with which he shoots his victims. The Latin word *cupido* means desire

681 **Idalium** a beautiful grove in Cyprus

682 **Cythera** Cythera is an island near Cyprus

693 **amaracus** thought to be the herb marjoram

734 **Bacchus** the Roman god of wine

740 **Iopas** Virgil's bard sings not of the great deeds of men as did the Homeric bards but of the wonders of nature, as he himself had done in the *Georgics* (see especially *Georgic* 2, lines 475–94)

741 **Atlas** there was a legend that he had been an astronomer

751 **Memnon, son of the Dawn** (see note on line 489). His arms were made by Vulcan, the god of fire

752 **Diomede** his horses had sprung from the sun, hence they breathed fire

BOOK 2   Aeneas tells Dido of the fall of Troy

Aeneas tells Dido how Troy was destroyed by the stratagem of the Wooden Horse and Sinon's deception. The spirit of Hector appears to Aeneas in a dream to tell him to leave the city taking with him the gods of Troy. Aeneas awakens to find Troy on fire. The Trojans offer resistance but are overwhelmed by the Greeks. Aeneas withdraws, carrying Anchises on his shoulders. He returns to search for Creusa, his wife, who has gone missing. Her spirit comes to him and tells him to journey to Italy.

Narrated from the Trojan point of view, the sack of Troy is not seen to be a great heroic feat of arms on the part of the Greeks but a pitiful horror story that is the result Greek treachery: Laocoon's sentiment 'I am afraid of Greeks, particularly when they bring gifts' (line 49) has become famously proverbial. Greek treachery is aided by Trojan folly and credulity. The Greeks are villains and the Trojans victims. We see events from the point of view of the defeated and the dispossessed.

In this retrospective narrative, overriding even the cunning deceit of Sinon is an oppressive sense of fate, first manifested in the monstrous sea serpents that engulf Laocoon and his sons as he is performing a sacrifice on the shore and which then take refuge in the temple of Athene. This the Trojans interpret as a divine sign of displeasure against Laocoon who dared to advise against accepting the Greek Horse and had thrown his spear at its side.

The appearance of Hector's mangled ghost to Aeneas confirms the doom of Troy and provides the first of many supernatural signs that it is Aeneas's destiny to leave the city and lead the Trojan remnant to new territory. These signs have to be powerful so that Aeneas cannot be charged with desertion. Even so, in the confusion that follows, he does not pay heed to this supernatural sign but leads a futile resistance, determined to die with the city.

The Trojans counter Greek treachery with a stratagem of their own when they attempt to confuse the enemy by donning the armour of dead Greeks, a stratagem that backfires when some of their number are killed by their own side. There are no heroics in what is a realistic account of a city's capture, just terror and confusion. The overwhelming power of the Greeks and its brutal effect are fully apparent in the attack upon the royal palace which results in the death of Priam (this features in Extended Commentaries, Text 1).

When Aeneas is distracted from thinking about his own family by the sight of Helen lurking in the temple of Vesta, Venus in turn distracts him from taking unheroic action by allowing him a vision of the gods energetically pulling down the walls of Troy, a further and more powerful supernatural sign which she follows by a divine order that he look to his family and leave.

Anchises's initial refusal to leave complicates the action and allows further expression to the patriotic desire to die in the fatherland while providing the necessary occasion for the third and final supernatural sign: the flame that appears as a halo effect around the young Iulus.

The image of Aeneas bearing Anchises on his shoulders, a practical demonstration of *pietas*, is one of the most famous in the poem. The loss of Creusa, necessitated by the demands of the plot so that Aeneas is free both to encounter Dido and to marry Lavinia, nevertheless has a **symbolic** effect discussed in Critical Approaches.

7 **Myrmidons** the followers of Achilles
the Dolopians were followers of the son of Achilles, Neoptolemos, or Pyrrhus as he is more frequently known

15 **Pallas Athene** offended by the judgement of Paris, Athene (also called by the Latin name Minerva at line 31), the virgin warrior goddess (she is depicted with spear, helmet and shield) helps in the plot against Troy

100 **Calchas** the leading Greek priest and prophet

104 **Ithaca** the island home of Ulysses

114 **the oracle of Phoebus** Phoebus meaning 'shining' is an **epithet** of Apollo; the false oracle refers to the sacrifice of Iphigeneia which the goddess Artemis demanded of Agamemnon her father before she would send favourable winds so that the Greeks could sail for Troy. Apollo was the chief Greek god of prophecy and his most famous oracle was at Delphi. His oracles were delivered through a human intermediary like the Sibyl (Book 6, lines 35–101)

132 **The sacred rites** coarse meal with salt was sprinkled on the sacrificial victim's head which was also decorated with headbands

183 **the Palladium** it was believed that Troy could not be taken as long as the Palladium (the image of the goddess Pallas, or Minerva) remained there

193 **Pelops** a grandson of Jupiter and grandfather of Agamemnon and Menelaus. The Peloponnese (Greece south of the Isthmus of Corinth) took its name from him

197 **Larisa** in Thessaly in northern Greece, as was Phthia, the kingdom of Achilles

270 **Hector** Troy's chief defender. He killed the Greek Patroclus who was wearing the borrowed armour of his friend Achilles (*Iliad*, Book 16). It was customary to strip a defeated opponent of his armour which then became the victor's spoils. In *Iliad*, Book 17 Hector sets fire to the Greeks' ships

296 **Vesta** see note in Book 1, line 292

343 **Cassandra** one of Priam's daughters. She was loved by Apollo, but resisted him. Consequently he rendered useless the gift of prophecy which he had imparted to her by causing her prophecies never to be believed

456 **Andromache** Hector's widow

457 **Astyanax** Hector's son, who was later thrown from the battlements of Troy by Ulysses

501 **Hecuba** Priam's wife and queen of Troy; the hundred women with her are the daughters and daughters-in-law of Priam, who had fifty sons and fifty daughters. Priam's great dynasty is extinguished. Aeneas, though related to Priam, is not his descendant

610 **Neptune** the earth shaker as well as the god of the sea. Here he helps to destroy the walls which he had himself helped to build. He had nursed a grievance against Troy after Laomedon, Priam's father, had cheated him of his payment for building the wall

612 **the Scaean Gate** this faced the sea and therefore the incoming Greeks

616 **Gorgon** the Gorgon was Medusa, who had been changed by Minerva into a hideous snake-haired creature, who had power to change into stone all who looked upon her. Her head was cut off by Perseus who then presented it to the goddess who in some representations had it on her shield

643 **one sack of the city** Troy had previously been sacked by Hercules

647 **hated by the gods** Anchises was blasted in a flash from Jupiter for boasting that he had slept with Venus. Venus had warned him to keep their love secret

693 **thunder ... on the left** regarded as a favourable sign by the Romans

694 **a star fell from the sky** reveals the way the Trojans are to leave and points in the direction of Mount Ida to the south-east of Troy

714 **Ceres** the old earth goddess, associated with agriculture

780 **a long exile** Creusa's prophecy is a clarification of the earlier prophecy spoken by Hector

781 **Hesperia** the western land, Italy, which is far west of Troy or Greece. Hesperus is the evening star which rises in the west. As they start their journey, the Trojans show no knowledge of this prophecy, an inconsistency possibly accounted for by the fact that the *Aeneid* was unfinished on Virgil's death

781 **the Lydian river Thybris** the Tiber flows through Rome, and it also flows by Etruria, and by tradition the Etruscans were Lydian in origin. Lydia is south of Troy

786 **I shall never go to be a slave** Creusa avoids slavery, the fate of the other Trojan women

788 **The Great Mother of the Gods** Cybele, a Phrygian goddess and patroness of Troy. She drives a chariot drawn by lions and her followers, the Corybantes, celebrate her godhead in dance and with clashing cymbals (see Book 3, lines 111–13 and Book 9, lines 614–20)

BOOK 3   **Aeneas tells the story of his seven years' wanderings from Troy**

There are four main episodes involving the fate of Polydorus, the encounter with the Harpies, the fate of Andromache and the tale of Achaemenides, prisoner of the Cyclopes. In Sicily Anchises dies. At various stages on his journey Aeneas is given oracles and prophecies, the chief of which is the speech of Helenus in Chaonia.

The wanderings of Aeneas are reminiscent of the wanderings of Odysseus from Troy, but while the Greek stories are romantic adventures which enhance the hero as he displays his superior prowess and ingenuity, those of Aeneas are full of horror and suffering in which Aeneas is largely a passive spectator or hearer. Anchises takes the lead in the interpretation of divine signs and prophecies.

By the time that Aeneas encounters Andromache her main physical suffering at the hands of the Pyrrhus are over; she is married to a Trojan, the prophet Helenus, and living quietly in a second (imitation) Troy. But as she offers libations to the spirit of the dead Hector, she is a ghostly figure and a tragic **symbol** of suffering. The story of Achaemenides is one of unmitigated horror; we hear the encounter with the monstrous Cyclops from the nonheroic point of view of the ordinary soldier left behind in the cave when Odysseus and the rest of his companions had escaped.

22 **spears of cornel and myrtle wood** cornel = dogwood. Myrtle is appropriate here as it is sacred to Venus to whom Aeneas is sacrificing. Aeneas prays to the nymphs of the countryside because such spirits are the guardians of woods and trees. There are also nymphs that dwell in mountains, the Oreads, and in the sea, the Nereids, and in fresh water, the Naiads

62 **we gave Polydorus a second burial** the first of many burials in the *Aeneid*. The Romans believed that if funeral rites were not properly performed, the soul of the departed could not be received amongst the spirits of the dead in Hades (see Book 6, line 325). The spirits are sometimes called 'shades'. The Latin word is *manes*

74 **the mother of the Nereids** Doris

92 **the sacred tripod** a three-legged stool upon which the priest of Apollo sat while awaiting inspiration from the god

94 **O much-enduring sons of Dardanus** the oracle of Apollo at Delphi was famous for the ambiguity of its utterances, and this oracle given to the Trojans at Delos is open to more than one interpretation. The Trojans are told to go to the country of their race's origin. Anchises takes this to

mean Crete, the home of Teucer, who was the first to settle on the site of
Troy. However, Dardanus, who built the first city of Troy, married Teucer's
daughter and he came from Italy. Anchises chooses the wrong branch of
the family

115 **Cnossus** the capital of Crete

122 **Idomeneus** on his return from Troy, Idomeneus, the leader of the Cretan
fleet, declared that he would sacrifice whatever he first encountered on his
landing. This proved to be his own son, and for this sacrifice he was
banished by the Cretans. He settled in Italy

131 **Curetes** priests of Jupiter in Crete. Mount Dicte on Crete was Jupiter's
birthplace

133 **Pergamea** another name for Troy

141 **The Dogstar** Sirius, which was present in the sky during the hottest part of
the Mediterranean summer

212 **Phineus** because he had blinded his own son the gods sent the Harpies to
torment him by continually carrying off his food

215 **Styx** the river of hate in Hades

239 **Misenus** the herald and trumpeter of Aeneas

248 **Laomedon** because he had cheated Neptune of his promised pay for helping
to build Troy's walls, his name was always associated with perjury

256 **deadly famine** see Book 7, line 109, for the fulfilment of Celaeno's
prophecy

272 **Ithaca** Laertes, the father of Ulysses (Odysseus), was in charge of the
kingdom of Ithaca in his son's absence. The wanderings of Ulysses
(narrated in Homer's *Odyssey*, Books 9, 11 and 12) were taking place at
the same time as those of Aeneas. There are many points of contact
between the two journeys, for instance, Scylla and Charybdis, the Cyclopes,
Circe's isle, the Harpies, Phaeacia and the Sirens' rocks

321 **the virgin daughter of Priam** Polyxena was loved by Achilles. As the Greeks
were about to sail home, the spirit of Achilles appeared to demand her
sacrifice. She was killed at the tomb of Achilles by Pyrrhus. See the *Hecuba*
of the Greek playwright Euripides (485–406BC)

331 **Orestes** the son of Agamemnon who together with his sister Electra killed
their mother Clytemnestra in revenge for her murder of Agamemnon. Orestes
was pursued by the Furies who avenge matricide: see the *Eumenides* ('The
Kindly Ones') by the Greek playwright Aeschylus (525–456BC); Hermione
was the daughter of Helen and Menelaus

346 **Helenus** the prophet of Apollo who understood the stars and astrology and could derive auguries (signs) from the cries of birds and auspices (signs) from their flight

350 **Xanthus** another name for the Scamander, a famous river that flowed by Troy

380 **Saturnian Juno** Saturn was the father of Juno and Jupiter

386 **the lakes of the underworld** Lake Avernus and the Lucrine Lake in Hades

390 **a great sow with the litter of thirty piglets** see Book 8, line 47. The thirty represent the thirty years between the founding of Lavinium by Aeneas and the founding of Alba Longa

420 **Scylla** Scylla and Charybdis represent the rocks and a whirlpool between Sicily and Italy (compare Homer's *Odyssey*, Book 12, line 94)

441 **Cumae** see Book 6, line 1. The prophetess is the Sibyl

537 **four horses** as at Carthage (Book 1, line 444) the horse is a sign of war, but as four white horses drew the chariot of the victor in a Roman triumph the omen suggests eventual triumph

578 **Enceladus** one of the giants who fought against Jupiter, who incapacitated him with his thunderbolt. The giants were immortal and so could not be killed. Most of them were imprisoned in Tartarus in Hades (see Book 6, lines 577–607)

641 **Polyphemus** Homer tells of the blinding of Polyphemus by Odysseus in *Odyssey*, Book 12. For the Cyclopes see Book 8, line 410

684 **Scylla and Charybdis** to avoid them the Trojans sail round Sicily

BOOK 4   Dido's love for Aeneas leads to disaster and her suicide

Dido confesses her love of Aeneas to her sister Anna, who advises her to marry him. While Dido and Aeneas are out hunting, Juno with the consent of Venus raises a storm which drives Aeneas and Dido into a cave where their love is consummated. Jupiter sends Mercury to order Aeneas to leave. Aeneas makes preparations and is confronted by Dido but remains deaf to her pleas. Aeneas leaves and Dido commits suicide.

The encounter of Dido embodies themes and raises issues that are central to the design of the poem which are discussed in Critical Approaches under Character.

6 **the lamp of Phoebus' sunlight** Apollo was also the god of the sun

20 **the death of my poor husband Sychaeus** for the history of this see Book 1, lines 338–70

26 **Erebus** one of the names for Hades

40 **Gaetulians ... Numidians** hostile neighbours. Dido emigrated from Sidon in Tyre or Phoenicia (see Book 1, lines 338–70)

41 **Syrtes** a large treacherous sandbank off the African coast

57 **as ritual prescribed** Dido is pious and meticulous in her devotions. She examines the inner organs of the animals for guidance. This was a common form of divination at Rome

95 **the arts of two gods** Juno's taunt recalls the trick of Venus in Book 1, lines 667–88

121 **beaters** men who went ahead of the main hunting party to drive the animals into the open

144 **like Apollo** in the spring Apollo returns from Lycia (in Asia Minor where he has a famous oracle) to his native Delos and leads the spring rites on Mount Cynthos where he was born. His followers from Crete, Parnassus (the Dryopes) and Scythia (the Agathyrsi) dance to his tune

165 **in the same cave** Juno had promised a marriage (line 99) and as goddess of marriage is there as *pronuba*, a matron who leads the bride to the bridal bed in a Roman marriage. The elements of earth, fire, air and water (the storm) participate in this natural marriage. The lightning is perhaps the marriage torch carried in procession at a Roman wedding; the air is witness and the mountain nymphs raise the wedding chant. Dido now considers herself married and later calls on Aeneas to honour their mutual pledge ('plighted hands', see lines 307 and 316). Aeneas denies (line 347) that he had entered into any solemn commitment

173 **Rumour** Coeus was a Titan, Enceladus a giant

215 **this second Paris** often regarded as an effeminate womaniser. Turnus similarly reproaches Aeneas for his perfumed hair at Book 12, line 100. See also the speech of Remulus at Book 9, lines 598–620

228 **twice rescued** Venus rescued Aeneas from Diomede (see *Iliad*, Book 5, line 311) and from Troy (*Aeneid*, Book 2, line 632)

242 **the rod** called a *caduceus*

247 **Atlas** described here both as the giant who held up the sky on his shoulders and as the mountain range in North Africa

301 **like a Bacchant** or Bacchanal; they are the female followers of Bacchus, the god of wine, who celebrated their god in riotous and ecstatic dancing by night. There was a famous festival of Bacchus held on Mount Cithaeron near Thebes (see Euripides's tragedy on this subject, the *Bacchae*). The Bacchanals surrendered to the intoxicating power of nature, abandoning the restraints of normal daytime living

367 **Caucasus** the Caucasus and Hyrcania are near the Caspian sea, a remote and inhospitable area as seen from Rome

426 **Aulis** the Greek fleet gathered here to sail for Troy

469 **Pentheus** the king of Thebes who was maddened by Dionysus. (See Euripides, *The Bacchae,* 918)

471 **Orestes** pursued by Furies after he had killed Clytemnestra, his mother

484 **Hesperides** maidens who lived on an island in the far west in which there was a garden of trees bearing golden apples which were guarded by a dragon

509 **the priestess ... called ... upon three hundred gods** this she does in solemn tones. Part of the ritual is the naming of all the powers of darkness by name, in order to avoid failure by neglecting any unnamed power. She names Erebus (Hades) and Chaos, and Hecate, a fearful infernal goddess who has three heads, one of a horse, one of a dog and another of a boar. Hecate is associated with witchcraft and is here identified with Diana the moon goddess. Diana is said to have three faces because she is identified not only with Hecate but also with Proserpina, queen of the underworld. The goddesses are identified with one another probably because they all operate in darkness

512 **water to represent the spring of Avernus** since this entrance to the underworld is near Lake Avernus (see Book 6, line 242) it is appropriate that water from this lake should be used in rites invoking the gods below

515 **a love charm, torn from the forehead of a new-born foal** there was a belief that a new-born foal had on its forehead a lump of flesh which the mother removed directly after birth. This was said to be useful as a love charm

625 **O my unknown avenger** the Carthaginian Hannibal, who invaded Italy and threatened Rome itself in the Punic War

BOOK 5   The Trojans mark the death of Anchises with funeral
          games in Sicily

Journeying from Carthage to Italy Aeneas is forced by a storm to land in
Sicily where he institutes funeral games on the anniversary of the death
of Anchises, with four main contests: a ship race, a boxing match, a foot
race and an archery contest. There follows an equestrian pageant led by
Ascanius. Weary of travel the Trojan women burn the ships. Aeneas
leaves them behind with Acestes and sets sail for Italy. His helmsman
Palinurus is lost on the journey.

> After the high tragedy of previous events, the funeral games
> which constitute most of this book provide a change of theme,
> tempo and atmosphere. Aeneas is more relaxed and seen for the
> first time in a paternal light, now that the elder father is no more.
> The games introduce Nisus and Euryalus whose friendship is
> prominent later in the poem in the **episode** of the night attack
> (Book 9). Here there is almost an element of comedy when Nisus
> who has slipped in the foot race trips up his nearest rival so that his
> friend Euryalus can win the race. Aeneas shows tact and fairness in
> dealing with the consequences. The glittering equestrian pageant
> led by Ascanius looks forward confidently to the next generation.
> But there is continuing trouble when the Trojan women burn the
> ships and the inexplicable death of the helmsman Palinurus effects
> a transition to the mood of the next book, the journey to the
> underworld.

84 **a snake slithered from under the shrine** a favourable omen. In the old Roman
   religion every natural thing (hill, tree, river) had its 'genius' or local spirit. It
   was frequently represented as a serpent, the **symbol** of renovation or new
   life. The soul of the dead, too, is often represented as a snake. Clearly the
   snake here represents the presence of Anchises at his tomb

118 *Chimaera* the ships are named after mythical beings. Chimaera is a fire
   breathing monster, part-dragon, part-lion, part-goat. A Centaur is half-man,
   half-horse. Scylla is described at Book 3, lines 425–8

248 **talent** a sum of money

370 **Paris** there was a tradition that he was a great boxer. He and Dares had
   fought in the funeral games for Hector

392 **Eryx** the son of Venus and father of Acestes, he had been killed by Hercules in a hand-to-hand fight. The leathers worn by Roman boxers on their hands were not for protection, but for the infliction of damage, since they were reinforced with metal. The boastful Dares gets what he deserves but clearly Virgil does not approve of the fight to the death that was obligatory in most Roman contests

523 **a mighty sign** the arrow catching fire anticipates the burning of the ships

549 **the horses drawn up** the equestrian pageant parallels the institution revived by Augustus and established by him on an annual basis, called the 'Troia'

588 **labyrinth** see Book 6, lines 14–30

637 **the image of the priestess Cassandra** the daughter of Priam and Hecuba who was carried off to Greece after the fall of Troy by Agamemnon, with whom she was subsequently murdered by Clytemnestra

658 **a great rainbow** Iris moves to and from the earth by way of a rainbow

723 **the form of his father Anchises** feels the approach of dawn when he must return to the shades below. Night and day both drive across the sky in a chariot

744 **to worship the Lar** every new decision or action is accompanied by religious ritual. In his own house, Aeneas invokes the spirits of Troy, most intimately concerned with the decision about Sicily or Italy

755 **Aeneas was ploughing the city bounds** this is the only detailed description of the founding of a city by Aeneas. It is appropriate in this book which is so concerned with propriety of ritual. It is a religious foundation to be protected by Venus and the spirit of his father

805 **you are born from it** Venus rose from the sea

808 **I who caught him up in a hollow cloud** Neptune rescued Aeneas from Achilles (see *Iliad*, Book 20, line 158)

864 **the Sirens' rocks** the Sirens' song charmed to destruction all who heard them (see *Odyssey*, Book 12, line 39)

BOOK 6   The descent into Hades

Having sailed up the Italian coast to Cumae, Aeneas goes to the temple of Apollo and receives the Sibyl's prophecy. She then acts as his guide on the journey to the underworld. They pass through the regions of darkness in which the souls of the dead await their doom until dismissed either to Tartarus, a place of punishment which the Sibyl describes to Aeneas, or to Elysium, where the spirits of the blessed dwell. Here Aeneas meets Anchises who explains the doctrine of the reincarnation of souls and shows him his Roman descendants.

The main purpose of this **episode** lies in the revelation given to Aeneas by Anchises of the illustrious Roman future. The climax of this and its aftermath are discussed in Text 2 of Extended Commentaries.

Anchises is in Elysium, the abode of the blessed. But two thirds of the book is concerned with ghastly and ghostly preliminaries: before he enters Hades Aeneas has to bury the body of Misenus, a comrade of whose recent death the Sibyl informs him. Once Hades is entered, Aeneas encounters the monsters and horrors of myth, meets the recently dead shades of Palinurus, of the unforgiving Dido and of the Trojan Deiphobus still in the mangled form in which he died at the hands of the Greeks on Troy's last night. Then comes the long account of the pains of Tartarus where the souls of the wicked are tormented eternally. Though the mood changes when they reach Elysium, Anchises's long speech ends with the lament for the death of Marcellus, so that the elegiac note returns.

10 **the awesome Sibyl** a name given to mythical prophetic women. This Sibyl is called Deiphobe. She lives in a cave and is inspired by Apollo, uttering truths when she is possessed by the god

13 **Diana** the moon goddess, identified with Hecate

14 **Daedalus** a legendary inventor and craftsman. He offended Minos, king of Crete and fled with his son Icarus with the aid of wings fastened together with wax. Icarus flew too near the sun which melted the wax so that he crashed to his death in the Icarian sea (part of the Aegean sea)

20 **Androgeos** son of Minos and Pasiphae, who won all the games at an Athenian festival, thereby exciting the jealousy of Aegeus, king of Athens, who killed him. Minos exacted from the Athenians an annual tribute of seven youths chosen by lot who were offered to the Minotaur. This was a monster, half-man half-bull, born to Pasiphae as a result of her union with a bull sent by Neptune, who was angry with Minos. The monster lived in the labyrinth, a maze built by Daedalus. One year later Theseus, son of Aegeus, went as one of the seven to try to set the Athenians free. Ariadne, daughter of Minos, fell in love with him and helped him to kill the Minotaur, giving him a ball of thread by which he was able to keep track of his way in the maze

56 **Phoebus Apollo** the most faithful of the gods in his support of the Trojan cause. At Troy, he directed Paris's arrow to the one part of Achilles's body that was vulnerable: his heel. Achilles's mother, the goddess Thetis, had tried to make him immortal by immersing him in the river Styx. She succeeded in making him invulnerable, with the exception of the ankle by which she held him. After Troy, Apollo aids the Trojans with oracles. The Sibyl is Apollo's priestess. After Jupiter and along with Mars he is the Olympian god most closely associated with Rome. The Romans had held games in honour of Apollo since the third century BC. Augustus built a marble temple to Apollo on the Palatine hill in which were kept the Sibylline books, ancient oracular utterances on the subject of Rome. Virgil associates both the games and the temple with the Trojan ancestor of Rome

74 **do not consign your prophecies to leaves** for the Sibyl's leaves, see Book 3, line 440

89 **A second Achilles** Turnus, also the son of Venilia, a nymph and so goddess-born. The Greek city is Pallanteum, home of Evander who will support Aeneas against Turnus

118 **Avernus** a volcanic lake near Cumae; its banks were forested

119 **Orpheus** the Thracian bard, who, in seeking to recover his wife Eurydice from the underworld, charmed the infernal powers with his lyre and song. At the gate of Hades he turned round to look at his wife, thereby breaking the condition upon which he had been permitted to leave with her. She was forced to return

121 **Pollux** was immortal, a son of Jupiter. His half-brother Castor was mortal. When Castor was killed, Pollux was allowed to spend half his time in Hades and half in heaven so that they could share immortality

Theseus he and his friend Pirithous tried to carry off Proserpina to the upper world. They appear later in Tartarus undergoing punishment for this (Book 6, lines 601, 617)

123 **Hercules** the hardest of his twelve labours was the task of fetching the dog Cerberus from Hades

132 **Cocytus** the four dreadful rivers of hell were Cocytus, Styx, Phlegethon and Acheron. They are all Greek names, which suggest, in turn, wailing, hate, fire and pain

137 **a golden bough** thought to have been an invention of Virgil's. Aeneas is led to it by a pair of doves, love-birds sacred to Venus. As Juno is queen of heaven, Proserpina is queen of Hades and therefore the Juno of the lower world. Given Juno's hostility to the Trojans, the mention of her name here makes the task seem even more formidable

153 **black cattle** black victims are offered to the powers below, white to the powers above

250 **the mother of the Furies** Night; her sister is Earth

285 **monstrous beasts** the **Centaurs** are half-horse half-man. For the **Scyllas** see Book 3, lines 420–32. **Briareus** has a hundred hands. The many-headed **Hydra** dwelt at Lerna near Argos and was slain by Hercules. The **Chimaera** was killed by Bellerophon. For the **Harpies** see Book 3, lines 209–62. **Geryon** was a giant killed by Hercules

334 **Orontes** see Book 1, line 113

337 **Palinurus** see Book 5, lines 833–71. Cape Palinurus is at the Bay of Paestum

402 **Proserpina** a daughter of Ceres and Jupiter. She was carried off to Hades by Pluto, king of the underworld and brother of Jupiter, who was therefore her uncle

432 **Minos** the judge in the underworld. He was the grandfather of the Minos mentioned earlier and a Cretan lawgiver

445 **Phaedra** the wife of Theseus, who killed herself for love of Hippolytus, her stepson

445 **Procris** she was suspicious of her husband, following him into the woods, where he accidentally killed her
Eriphyle was bribed with a beautiful necklace to induce her husband to fight against Thebes. As he died there he asked his sons to kill their mother. This Amphion later did

447 **Evadne** wife of Capaneus, another of the seven heroes who attacked Thebes. He was struck by lightning for his impiety and Evadne threw herself upon his funeral pyre
Pasiphae see note to line 20, under 'Androgeos'
Laodamia wife of Protesilaus, who died with her husband after he had been allowed to return for three hours from the dead

448 **Caeneus** originally a man, changed into a woman by Neptune

479 **Tydeus** he, Parthenopaeus, and Adrastus were three of the heroes who attacked Thebes (before the Trojan War). The rest of the warriors are Trojans killed in the war. Idaeus was Priam's charioteer

495 **Deiphobus** as the oldest surviving son of Priam, he married Helen after the death of Paris. Helen is seen by him as by Aeneas earlier as a treacherous harlot who had betrayed both sides

505 **Cape Rhoeteum** north of Troy

543 **Tartarus** the place of punishment

555 **Tisiphone** her name means she who avenges murder. She is one of the Furies

580 **the army of Titans** giant sons of Heaven and Earth, an older generation of gods who were thrown out of heaven by Jupiter and the new generation of Olympians

Sons of Aloeus Otus and Ephialtes. They had threatened the gods by piling Ossa on Olympus and Pelion on Ossa (all mountains). They were defeated by Apollo

585 **Salmoneus** dared to rival Jupiter

595 **Tityos** a giant who was killed by Apollo for assaulting his mother Latona

601 **the Lapiths** Ixion was their king, and, having been taken into heaven by Jupiter, tried to win the love of Juno

Pirithous he and Theseus were punished for attempting to abduct Proserpina

618 **Phlegyas** set fire to the temple of Apollo

630 **the Cyclopes** monsters who made Jupiter's thunderbolts and forged the battlements of Tartarus

645 **Orpheus** legendary poet and seer who sang to the accompaniment of the lyre. He is regarded as a bringer of civilisation and is associated with knowledge of the lower world (Orphism). In Latin the word *vates* means both poet and prophet

659 **Eridanus** the river Po

667 **Musaeus** son of Orpheus, another mythical bard

763 **Silvius** Anchises shows Aeneas the Alban kings. Alba Longa was founded by Ascanius but its kings were descended from Aeneas's son by Lavinia, Silvius, so called because he had been born in a wood. All the places mentioned had been fortified by the Alban kings

768 **Numitor** the father of Ilia, mother of Romulus

772 **the Civic Crowns** a wreath of oak given to anyone who had saved a fellow countryman's life in battle

779 **the double crest** a twin-crested helmet is an emblem of Mars

784 **the Mother Goddess of Mount Berecyntus** Cybele, otherwise known as Rhea,

mother of Jupiter and other gods, who was worshipped in Phrygia near
Mount Berecyntus and Mount Dindyma. She was carried around in a chariot
adorned by a battle crown, as she invented the art of fortifying cities. She is
associated therefore with the development of civilisation and especially with
Troy (see Book 9, lines 70 and 617)

789 **Caesar** the Caesars are mentioned here to be associated with Rome's
founder, Romulus. After his death, Julius Caesar was deified. Augustus took
the epithet '*divus*', the divine, in his own lifetime. Saturn was thought to
have reigned over Latium in the Golden Age (see Book 8, line 319)

794 **Garamantes** one of Augustus's generals conquered this African people in
19BC, the year of Virgil's death

796 **Atlas** the Atlas mountains in North Africa

799 **the kingdoms round Lake Maeotia** territory near the Sea of Azov

801 **Hercules** he travelled from country to country as he performed his twelve
labours. He pursued the Arcadian deer for a year before capturing it. He
caught a monstrous boar in the wood of Erymanthus, and destroyed the
Hydra (see note to line 285). Hercules was one of the great heroes of
achievement with whom Augustus was closely associated by poets

805 **triumphing Bacchus** brought up by the nymphs of Mount Nysa in India, he
travelled all over the world in a chariot drawn by tigers

810 **the Roman king called from the ... town of Cures** Numa; many Roman
institutions were attributed to him

814–5 **Tullus ... Ancus** also kings of Rome

817 **the Tarquin kings** Tarquin, Rome's last king, murdered Brutus's brother,
whereupon Brutus incited the Romans to expel the Tarquins. The expulsion
of the kings heralded the Roman Republic. The Latin word for the rods of
office is *fasces* (a bundle of rods with an axe). They were always associated
with Rome's chief magistrates, the consuls. The sons of Brutus tried to
restore the kings but Brutus ordered their execution. He was an ancestor of
Marcus Brutus, one of the conspirators who assassinated Julius Caesar

824 **the Decii** one of the great families of the Roman Republic. They died
fighting for Rome, the father against the Latins, the son against the Gauls

825 **Torquatus** so named from the *torques* or necklace: a spoil of war taken from
a gigantic Gaul killed by him in single combat. He also executed his son for
disobeying orders

Camillus one of the great heroes of the Roman Republic, Camillus defeated
the Gauls, Etruscans and Volscians

830 **the father-in-law ... the son-in-law** Pompey who married Caesar's daughter Julia. Caesar made war on Pompey by crossing the Rubicon with the legions with which he had conquered Gaul. They fought at Pharsalus. Pompey fled to Egypt in defeat and was ignominiously murdered there

836 **the man who will triumph over Corinth** Mummius was granted a triumph for the conquest of Greece

838 **the man who will raze Argos** Aemilius Paulus, the conqueror of Macedon in northern Greece. Troy through Rome reverses its defeat in the Trojan War (see Book 1, lines 283–5)

840 **the shrine of Minerva** desecrated on the night of Troy's fall by the theft of the Palladium and by Ajax (see Book 1, line 41)

841 **Cato** (234–149BC) an austere and conservative Roman who resisted the new era of luxury brought in by Roman conquest of the East
Cossus winner of the highest award in the Roman state, the *spolia opima* reserved for those who killed an enemy general

842 **the Gracchi** two famous brothers who as tribunes (representatives) of the people attempted to reform the Roman state. Their father fought with distinction in Spain

843 **the Scipios** Scipio Africanus Major defeated Hannibal at the battle of Zama in 202BC. His adopted grandson captured Carthage in 146BC and made Africa a Roman province

844 **Fabricius** a general who fought against the Greeks, and a famous example of the old Roman virtue. He was incorruptible and despised wealth
Serranus Cincinnatus, an early Roman hero who cultivated his farm with his own hands and was reportedly sowing his fields when he was told that he had been elected consul, the highest office of the Roman state

845 **Fabius Maximus** the most famous of this illustrious family, who commanded the Roman army after its defeat by Hannibal at Cannae. By skilful use of delaying tactics he wore Hannibal down and saved Rome from defeat

847 **Others** the Greeks who excelled the Romans in sculpture, literature and the sciences

855 **Marcellus** a famous Roman general who fought against the Carthaginians and put down a rebellion in southern Gaul. He won the *spolia opima*, only the third Roman to do so after Romulus and Cossus. A descendant of this Marcellus married Augustus's sister Octavia. Their son, called Marcellus, married Augustus's daughter Julia and was designated Augustus's successor. However, he died in 23BC at the age of twenty. He was buried in

BOOK 6 continued

a Mausoleum which Augustus had built five years before on the Campus Martius by the Tiber

895 **the Gate of Ivory** there is no obvious reason why Virgil makes Aeneas return to the upper world by way of the gate of false dreams

BOOK 7   **Aeneas lands in Italy, is welcomed by Latinus but opposed by Turnus. War breaks out. Forces are mustered**

Aeneas lands in Latium and sends envoys to Latinus who recognises him as the stranger who the oracle Faunus has foretold will marry Lavinia. Latinus welcomes the Trojans. Juno causes the Fury Allecto to stir up opposition to Aeneas. She maddens Amata and provokes Turnus. Fighting breaks out over the killing of a stag. Preparations for war are made and the muster of Latin forces is described.

When the Trojans arrive, they see the sturdy Latin youth engaged in chariot racing, exercising on horseback and practising energetic sports (lines 160–5). They find Latinus enthroned in a grand building that is both a palace and a temple surrounded by wooden images of his ancestors which represent the spirit of old Italy (lines 169–91). There is father Sabinus, planter of the vine, with his pruning hook, Saturn and Janus, Picus the tamer of horses, and other kings who have suffered wounds for their country. On the massive gates of the building are hung the memorials of war, including captive chariots, curved axes, helmet crests, javelins and shields. The temple is grand but austere with none of the bronze work or delicate artistry of the temple of Juno in Carthage; as well as enshrining the spirit of old Italy, it is a testament to its war-like history. Latinus himself is a descendant of Faunus who was the god of agriculture and cattle (line 47). In Latium therefore the Trojans encounter the austere agrarian community which was the basis for early Roman society.

The outbreak of war is represented as something hellish by the clear **symbolism** of the device whereby Juno raises the Fury Allecto from the underworld to infect the Latins with her maddening poison, thereby breaking the peace (lines 312–560). With war comes monstrous unreason. At the same time that the occasion of the outbreak should be a comparatively trivial incident involving the stag complements the symbolism with realism.

The martial spirit of the indigenous peoples from whom the Romans derive their language and institutions is celebrated in the catalogue of forces with which the book ends. The chief representatives of that spirit, Turnus, Mezentius and Camilla, even in defeat to some extent embody the Italian strength and courage upon which Roman power is to depend (see Book 12, line 827).

10 **Circe** Helenus had predicted that Aeneas would visit this island (Book 3, line 386). Circe was a minor goddess who had magical powers; she could change men into animals and changed some of the companions of Ulysses into pigs (see *Odyssey*, Book 10)

37 **Erato** one of the nine Muses who lived on Mount Helicon, goddesses of inspiration who presided over the various arts and sciences. Erato was usually the goddess of love poetry. Perhaps she is invoked here because the war was fought for the hand of Lavinia in marriage. The invocation introduces the second half of the poem said by the poet to be grander

48 **Faunus ... Picus** both had prophetic powers. Faunus, apart from being a god of agriculture and cattle, was also one of the great founders of the religion of the country. Worship of him continued in Virgil's time

49 **Saturn** according to legend, the original inhabitants of Italy were country spirits, fauns and nymphs. The god Saturn was the first king of Latium which he civilised and reigned over during the Golden Age (Book 8, lines 314–29)

59 **a laurel tree** especially venerated at Rome. Priam had similarly built his altars around a laurel at Troy (Book 2, line 513)

85 **Oenotria** an ancient name for a region of Italy

116 **We are eating even our tables** Celaeno's prophecy (see Book 3, lines 255–7). The Trojans eat their cakes of meal which they had been using as 'tables' on which they put their fruit

154 **Pallas Athene's olive wreathed in wool** carried in the hand, they are a sign of peace, the olive being sacred to Minerva

173 **rods of office** the *fasces* carried in procession before the consuls. The palace is also a temple where the king's power is sanctified

178 **Italus** not strictly an ancestor of Latinus, but a king associated with a different part of Italy (which took its name from him)

178 **Sabinus** ancestor of the Sabines, a neighbouring people

180 **Janus** a native Roman god of the doorway who therefore faced both
ways (for the gates of Janus see Book 1, line 294 and Book 7,
lines 607–17)

189 **Picus** he wears a Roman toga (note that the Trojans wear unfamiliar dress)
and holds the sacred *lituus* or augury-staff. Romulus was an augur (one who
foretold future events from the flight or other action of birds) and founded
Rome by use of this art. Hence the augur's staff is called Quirinal, Quirinus
being the name of Romulus when deified. Picus had been turned into a bird
by Circe. His name in Latin means woodpecker

206 **the Auruncan elders** the Auruncans are regarded as a primitive people, the
original inhabitants of Italy. From them came the story of Dardanus's
emigration to Troy (see Book 3, line 96)

226 **the stream of Oceanus** was supposed to encircle the earth

294 **Sigean** Trojan

304 **Mars …Lapiths** he was the only god not invited to the wedding of their king
Perithous. He took revenge by starting the quarrel between the Lapiths and
the Centaurs

306 **Calydon … Diana** she destroyed the whole city because their king had
omitted to sacrifice to her when he sacrificed to all the other gods (see
Iliad, Book 9, line 533)

319 **Bellona** the war goddess will be the *pronuba*, the matron who brings the
bride to the bedchamber

320 **Hecuba** Priam's wife Hecuba dreamed that she was pregnant with a burning
torch before she gave birth to Paris. The torch was a portent of the
destruction of Troy and perhaps of the marriage that led to it

324 **Allecto** one of the Furies whose Greek name suggests implacability

341 **the poisons of the Gorgons** the three Gorgons were snake-haired

363 **the Phrygian shepherd** Paris, who was tending sheep when asked to make
his famous judgement

371 **the house of Turnus** Inachus and Acrisius were kings of Argos. The daughter
of Acrisius, Danae, emigrated from Greece to Italy, built the town of Ardea
and married Pilumnus by whom she became mother of Daunus, the father
of Turnus (see line 410)

390 **the soft-leaved thyrsus** carried by Bacchus and his followers, a straight staff
topped with a pine cone or a bunch of vine leaves and grapes or ivy leaves
and berries

487 **Silvia** means 'of the woods'. The son of Aeneas by Lavinia was to be called Silvius. Rhea Silvia or Ilia was the mother of Romulus

604 **the Getae, the Hyrcani, or the Arabs** all peoples beyond the bounds of the Roman empire

606 **Parthians** Roman standards (*signa*, the equivalent of modern regimental flags) had been surrendered by Crassus to the Parthians in 53BC. One of Augustus's generals had recovered them, salvaging Roman honour

617 **Gates of War** see also Book 1, line 294. The consul wore special robes for this ceremonial. The cincture was formed by pulling the toga tight around the body. The connection with Gabii is unexplained

642 **what kings were roused to war** Homer has a similar catalogue in *Iliad*, Book 2

656 **Hercules** for the legends about him, see notes to Book 8

762 **Virbius** Hippolytus's stepmother was Phaedra who fell in love with him and, when he did not respond to her advances, falsely accused him before his father Theseus of making advances to her. Theseus requested his father Poseidon to destroy him. The god sent a bull from the sea to frighten the horses of Hippolytus as he rode along the shore in his chariot

789 **Io** was a beautiful maiden loved by Jupiter. He turned her into a cow to avoid Juno's suspicions. Juno requested the cow as a present which Jupiter felt bound to give her. Juno set Argus, a creature with a hundred eyes, to keep watch over Io

BOOK 8   Aeneas visits Pallanteum (the site of Rome) in search of allies. He is presented with a divinely made shield

Having sailed up the Tiber, Aeneas finds Evander holding a feast in honour of Hercules. Evander welcomes him and tells him the story of Hercules and Cacus. Aeneas is shown round the kingdom of Evander, the site of future Rome. Venus procures arms for her son. There is an elaborate description of the shield.

The austerity of the scene in which Evander invites Aeneas to join their simple feast is matched by an austerity in Virgil's description. There are, for example, no **similes**. Much is made of the contrast between the humble origins of the city (where oxen low on the site of the Forum) and Rome's future greatness and wealth, with implied criticism of Roman extravagance and ostentation. But the scene and setting also bring out differences between the culture and civilisation of the Trojans and the austere simplicity of Italian life. 'You too must have the courage to despise wealth' (line 364), Evander bids Aeneas. Typically, Virgil suppresses the reaction of his hero. Although he is a happy and interested listener and spectator, Aeneas is a stranger at Pallanteum and the scene obliquely underlines what he has lost in coming to settle in Italy.

The significance of the shield is discussed in Critical Approaches, on The *Aeneid* as an Epic of Rome.

9 **the city of great Diomede** Argyripa. For the results of this embassy see Book 9, lines 225–95

31 **Tiber** like most rivers it is personified as an old man. River gods are represented by bull's horns suggesting strength or noise (line 77)

44 **a great sow** see Book 3, lines 388–92. Tiber adds to the prophecy of Helenus the name of the second town, Alba, and the significance of the number thirty (see also Book 1, line 230)

51 **Pallas** a Greek hero who lived in Arcadia in southern Greece. His descendant Evander emigrated from Greece and settled on the site of Rome which he called Pallanteum from the old Arcadian city of that name. The name of the Palatine Hill at Rome marks the connection with Pallas (see Book 6, line 97 for the Sibyl's prophecy of aid from a Greek city for Aeneas)

103 **Hercules** the son of Alcmene, wife of Amphitryon. His real father was Jupiter. Hercules, a popular Roman god, was worshipped at the great altar near the Aventine hill at Rome. As a hero who triumphed over difficult tasks he is associated with victory

134 **Dardanus** see Book 1, line 380 and Book 3, line 165

140 **Atlas** compare Book 6, line 247

146 **the Rutulians of king Daunus** Daunus was the father of Turnus

158 **Priam** Hesione was married to the Greek Telamon, father of Ajax. Priam made his journey before the abduction of Helen when Greeks and Trojans were on friendly terms as they are now to be again

166 **Lycian arrows** the Lycians were famous bowmen

181 **the gift of Ceres** bread

194 **Cacus** the worship of Hercules is the first ritual encountered in Italy that is not connected with native Italian gods, Hercules having been a Greek hero. The story of Cacus, however, connects him with the region and makes him a

Roman hero. He is shown in characteristic light, using his strength in the cause of order and justice, ridding the earth of a monster who held the locality in fear. He was returning from Spain where he had disposed of Geryon, a monster with three heads (see Book 6, line 289)

269 **Potitius ... and the Pinarii** two ancient Roman families

285 **the Salii** usually twelve priests of Mars but here identified with Hercules. Hercules was the son of Jupiter, as was Mars. These three gods preside over the martial and ruling spirit of the Roman state

289 **the two snakes** Hercules was the product of one of Jupiter's affairs. The jealous Juno, his stepmother, sent two snakes to kill the infant who strangled them in his cradle

291 **Troy and Oechalia** Neptune had sent a sea monster against the Trojans. Hercules killed it but when cheated of his promised reward sacked Troy. Eurytus was king of Oechalia and promised his daughter Iole to the winner of an archery contest. Hercules won but was refused Iole. Therefore he sacked the city and carried her off

a thousand labours Eurystheus was king of Tiryns whom Hercules had to serve for twelve years by decree of the gods. The king set him twelve tasks, known as the 'Labours of Hercules', several of which are now celebrated. The **Centaurs** were descended from Ixion and a cloud. They had the form of a man from the waist up and of a horse from the waist down. Hercules was drinking with the centaur **Pholus** when he was attacked by the others, several of whom he killed, including **Hylaeus**. Hercules saved Crete from a bull driven mad by Neptune. He strangled a lion which was terrorising **Nemea**, a valley in Argolis. He was sent to bring Cerberus up from Hades (see Book 6, line 417). He joined in the war against the Giants. **Typhoeus** was a hundred-headed fire-breathing monster. At Lerna Hercules grappled with the **Hydra**, a many-headed monster which grew two new ones for every one cut off. Hercules finally burnt them off

314 **native fauns and nymphs** see Book 7, line 45

319 **Saturn** see Book 6, line 792. He is spoken of as an exile so that he may be associated with Aeneas

338 **Carmental Gate** south-west of the Capitol

342 **Asylum** there is a tradition that Romulus opened a refuge for immigrants at Rome to increase the size of the city

343 **Lupercal** a cavern in the Palatine connected with Evander and the Arcadian worship of Pan, the nature god

345 **Argiletum** north-east of the Forum. One of Evander's guests, Argos, was killed here for conspiring against his host. In Virgil's time it was a trading centre

347 **the Capitol** the highest of Rome's seven hills and centre of the city on which were several temples to the gods. The Tarpeian rock was nearby

354 **aegis** the whirlwind which drove the storm cloud. It was also the breastplate of Jupiter

358 **Janiculum** a hill on the west side of the Tiber. There was a tradition that on it were the remains of an old city where Janus had reigned jointly with Saturn who had a similar city on the Capitol called **Saturnia**

361 **the Roman Forum** the legal and deliberative centre of Rome
the Carinae a fashionable and luxurious quarter of Rome mentioned here to contrast with the simple poverty of Evander's settlement

383 **Thetis, the daughter of Nereus** Thetis, mother of Achilles who also begged Vulcan to make divine armour for her son (see *Iliad*, Book 18, line 421)

384 **the wife of Tithonus** Aurora, the dawn. Vulcan made arms for her son Memnon (see Book 1, line 489)

416 **Lipari** the Lipari islands are a group of volcanic islands north-east of Sicily where Vulcan had his forge. For the **Cyclopes** see Book 3, line 637. The **Chalybes** are a people in Pontus supposed to be the inventors of iron-working

454 **Lemnos** Vulcan was hurled from heaven by Jupiter and fell all day before landing upon Lemnos, an island in the Aegean, afterwards sacred to him

479 **the warlike Lydians** there was a tradition that the Etruscans were Lydian in origin. Lydia is south of Troy

498 **an aged prophet** a *haruspex*, one who foretells future events from the inspection of the entrails of sacrificial victims. This was a practice of Etruscan origin (compare Book 4, lines 63–4)

506 **Tarchon** the ruler who succeeded Mezentius

561 **walls of Praeneste** a few miles south-east of Rome

635 **the rape of the Sabines** according to the Roman historian Livy, Rome was short of women, and overtures to the neighbouring Sabines asking for intermarriage had been refused. Accordingly games were held to which the Sabines were invited. At a pre-arranged signal the Romans seized the Sabine maidens and carried them off. **Tatius** was king of the Sabines and lived at Cures. War broke out between the two nations which was halted by the intervention of the Sabine women

642 **Mettus** dictator of Alba; he was summoned by the Romans under Tullus
Hostilius as an ally against a neighbouring foe. He withdrew his troops in
the midst of the fighting. Later the Albans were disarmed by the victorious
Romans and Mettus was torn to pieces for his desertion by chariots driven
in opposing directions

646 **Porsenna** an Etruscan king who tried to force the exiled king Tarquin back
on the Romans who in turn resisted with force. **Horatius Cocles** defended the
bridge over the Tiber against the Etruscans until it was cut down under him.
Cloelia was given to Porsenna as hostage and escaped by swimming the
Tiber

652 **Manlius** in 390BC the Gauls had entered Rome and were attempting to
capture the Capitol. The consul Manlius was awakened by cackling geese
and was able to repel the Gauls

663 **Salii** see note on line 285; they have sacred shields
Luperci priests of the nature god Pan. At his festival they ran about half
naked, with sheepskin headdresses, and holding goatskin thongs

665 **chaste matrons** they gave their gold to Camillus who had vowed a temple to
Apollo if he took Veii. Their reward was to ride in sacred processions in four-
wheeled chariots with cushions

667 **Tartarus** the place of punishment in Hades (see Book 6, line 556)

668 **Catiline** in 63BC he headed a conspiracy against the government which was
defeated by Cicero. A notorious traitor

670 **Cato** the younger Cato, an austere stoic like the elder Cato. He committed
suicide in the Roman manner after Pompey had been defeated by Caesar

678 **Augustus Caesar** the climactic scene is the battle of Actium fought in 31BC
by Augustus (then Octavian) against Mark Antony and Cleopatra. **Agrippa**
was Augustus's general. He won the Naval Crown on which were represented
the 'beaks' of the ships involved in the battle. A decisive factor was
Cleopatra's desertion. The battle is represented as a clash between Western
Roman gods and Oriental deities such as Anubis, an Egyptian god with the
head of a dog. As the saviour of Roman values and the restorer of peace,
Augustus was granted a Roman triumph (a ceremonial procession through
the city) for victories over Dalmatia in 34–33BC, Actium, 31BC, and
Alexandria, 30BC. He built a temple to Apollo on the Palatine in 28BC and is
here represented as being seated on the threshold receiving gifts from
conquered nations from various parts of the world: Africa (Numidians), Asia
Minor (Lelegeians and Carians), Northern Europe (Gelonians and the Morini

BOOK 8 continued

on the North Sea). He reasserted Roman control over the Euphrates (in Asia Minor), the Rhine (Northern Europe) and the Araxes (in Armenia) which was conquered by a new bridge

BOOK 9   The Trojans are besieged. Nisus and Euryalus attack the enemy at night

The Rutulians led by Turnus besiege the Trojan camp. At night Nisus and Euryalus try to warn Aeneas but are killed in the attempt. The siege continues and Turnus distinguishes himself in the fighting.

The nocturnal adventure of Nisus and Euryalus is one of the most famous **episodes** in the poem. Virgil tells the story in such a way as to celebrate their friendship and devotion to one another (Euryalus will not let Nisus go alone, and Nisus dies trying to save his friend). They are the subject of a unique **apostrophe** by Virgil: 'Fortune has favoured you both! If there is any power in my poetry, the day will never come when time will erase you from the memory of man' (line 446ff.). Despite this, there can be no doubt that their death is a consequence of their excesses as they indulge in indiscriminate slaughter and greedy desire for plunder. The patriotic impulse is undermined by the emotions unleashed with it. There is great **pathos** in the figure of the mother of Euryalus. Her lamentation bears witness to the human cost of war to those who are the innocent victims of it.

5 **Thaumas** means in Greek 'a marvel'. Iris was his daughter. He was the son of Ocean and Earth

10 **Corythus** founder of Cortona in Etruria. The cities of Corythus therefore are the Etruscan cities whose troops Evander had offered to Aeneas (Book 8, lines 478–519)

102 **Galatea and Doto** sea nymphs, daughters of the sea god Nereus

104 **Styx** to swear by Styx, the river of hate in Hades, was the most solemn oath man or god could make (see Book 6, line 324)

176 **Nisus** see also Book 5, lines 315–61

218 **Acestes** see Book 5, line 715, where Aeneas leaves behind the women and the old in Sicily

264 **Arisba** a city near Troy. The conquest must have been before the Trojan War

303 **Lycaon of Cnossus** Cnossus is the capital of Crete. Cretan arms were famous

405 **daughter of Latona** Diana. Nisus had dedicated 'trophies' to her after hunting expeditions

496 **Tartarus** here simply the underworld

505 **in tortoise formation** the siege tactics here, with scaling ladders and the *testudo*, the tortoise formation, are those of Virgil's day. The tortoise formation provided the ancient equivalent of an armoured tank. A large number of soldiers would form a square. Those in the middle raised their shields above their heads. Those on the sides used their long shields to cover their bodies. Provided they kept to the formation the soldiers were thus protected against all but the heaviest missiles

525 **Calliope** chief of the nine Muses, and Muse of **epic** poetry

564 **the eagle, the armour-bearer of Jupiter** it was believed to carry his thunderbolts. The eagle was also a **symbol** of Roman power

599 **You have been sacked twice already, you Phrygians** once by Hercules and then by the Greeks. Remulus like Turnus (Book 9, lines 152–5) presents himself as an honest adversary in contrast to the cunning and treacherous Greeks. He represents the old Roman ideal of straightforward manliness, toughly disciplined against any adversary whether natural or human. He scorns Phrygian effeminacy, mocking their colourful dress (compare Iarbas at Book 4, line 215) and their love of dancing, music and song

BOOK 10   The death of Pallas

In an acrimonious council of the gods, Jupiter withdraws, leaving all to the fates. Aeneas returns from Pallanteum with substantial forces. In the subsequent fighting Pallas is killed by Turnus. Aeneas reacts savagely, killing Lausus and Mezentius.

Jupiter's bafflement at the direction in which events are going because of the opposition between Venus and Juno comes as a strong contrast to the certainty with which he had proclaimed his Olympian view in Book 1. The council confirms that whatever the long view, the ways in which the fates are actually worked out through human agency are complicated and circuitous. The council also marks an important stage in the poem; the death of Pallas is the pivotal event upon which the plot of the second half turns.

The **pathos** invested in the death of the Trojans and their allies (Nisus and Euryalus previously and Pallas here) is extended to the Italians too with the death of Lausus and Mezentius, in which the central value of the poem, *pietas*, has a part to play.

12 **Carthage** Hannibal invaded Italy in 218BC and threatened Rome itself

29 **Diomede** see Book 8, line 9 where the Latins sent envoys to Diomede, now settled in Apulia. Diomede had wounded Venus in the arm with his spear at *Iliad*, Book 5, line 336

51 **Amathus** Amathus, Idalium and Paphos are all in Cyprus

76 **Venilia** a sea nymph

97 **As Juno was making her plea** given the way the gods work, there is some logic in what Juno has just said. She is only trying to help her favourite as Venus is trying to help her son

113 **The Fates will find their way** Jupiter, like Latinus, stands back to let events take their course. The nod and oath are a repetition of Book 9, lines 104–6

157 **Phrygian lions** the ram or beak (*rostrum*) was the curved end of the ship's prow, often painted. The lions are an ornament attached to the beak. The protectress of the Trojan fleet was Cybele, the Phrygian goddess, who was carried in a chariot drawn by lions (see Book 3, lines 111–33)

186 **Cunarus** he and **Cupavo** were sons of **Cycnus** who was devoted to **Phaethon**, and when Phaethon was killed by a thunderbolt from Jupiter (because he dared to drive the chariot of the sun) Cycnus, weeping for his fate, was changed into a swan. The sisters of Phaethon who had helped him by yoking the horses to the chariot were also changed into swans

216 **Phoebe** Diana, as Apollo her brother was Phoebus

273 **Sirius the Dogstar** fiery because its rising was the sign for hot weather (dog days)

319 **the weapons of Hercules** he was Evander's guest when he fought against Cacus (see Book 8, line 203)

493 **Whatever honour there is in a tomb** Turnus observes the proprieties of battle by granting his enemy burial. It is also acceptable to strip a defeated enemy of his armour which becomes the legitimate spoil of war. Pallas (Book 10, line 450) had hoped to do the same to Turnus. However, it is the sight of Pallas's belt on Turnus that brings about his own death (see Book 12, lines 945–6). Aeneas in anger would deny Tarquitus (Book 10, line 550) burial, but he relents in the case of Lausus and does not despoil him

565 **Aegaeon** one of the giants who rebelled against Jupiter

581 **the horses of Diomede** Aeneas had been rescued from Diomede by Venus

761 **the Fury Tisiphone** see Book 6, line 555

763 **Orion** a giant hunter, who, having lost his sight, was told that he would regain it if he went to the east to meet the rising sun. He would use the tree for his club

815 **the Fates** the Parcae who spin the threads of life, allot them and finally cut them off

BOOK 11   The dead are buried and the war is renewed

Funeral ceremonies are performed for Pallas. The Latins hold a council to debate whether the war should be continued. The fighting is renewed and centres upon the exploits of Camilla.

The strain of lamentation with which this book begins is continued when Diomede recounts the misfortunes of the Greeks returning from Troy and confesses to the envoys of Turnus that he does not recall his part in the Trojan War with any pleasure. Homeric heroism is undercut by Virgil here.

The debates in the council that follows are a reflection of the uncertainty and discord that war brings in its wake.

The progress of Camilla is described by Virgil with great energy and vigour, but for all her noble ferocity and the favour she enjoys with Diana she is undone when, intent on possessing the gold armour of her Phrygian foe, she throws all caution to the winds. Camilla's spirited daring is taken to excess and leads to folly.

243 **we have seen Diomede** ambassadors had been sent at Book 8, line 9 to Argyripa in Apulia on the eastern coast of Italy to seek the aid of Diomede against the Trojans whom he had fought in the Trojan War. Argyripa takes its name from Argos of which Diomede had been king

247 **Garganus** a mountain in Apulia, a region in south-eastern Italy

253 **Ausonians** Ausonia is an old name for Italy

259 **Priam** a reversal of Book 2, line 6 where Aeneas says that even the followers of Ulysses would pity the sufferings of the Trojans

the deadly star of Minerva refers to the storm which she sent to scatter the Greek fleet (see Book 1, line 38 and *Odyssey*, Book 3, line 132)

260 **rocks of Euboea and Caphereus** Nauplius, king of Euboea, wrecked the Greek
fleet on its return from Troy because his son Palamedes had been
condemned to death by the Greeks before Troy. In revenge Nauplius hung
out false lights over the dangerous headland of Caphereus

262 **Proteus** Menelaus was driven to the isle of Pharos off the Egyptian coast
where he found the Egyptian sea king Proteus (see *Odyssey*, Book 4, line
354)

263 **Ulixes** Ulysses's adventure in the cave of Polyphemus is told in *Odyssey*,
Book 11 and recalled by Achaemenides at Book 3, lines 613–54

264 **Neoptolemus** he was killed by Orestes (see Book 3, line 325)

265 **Idomeneus** he was expelled from Crete
Locrians followed Ajax, son of Oileus, who was killed by Minerva (see Book
1, line 41). They subsequently drifted to the African coast

266 **the leader of the great Achivi** Agamemnon, who was murdered on his return
by his wife Clytemnestra and her lover Aegisthus

270 **Calydon** in Aetolia, the ancient home of Diomede. His father Tydeus had
migrated to Argos. His wife according to some accounts left him for
another. The reason for the transformation of his comrades into birds here is
not known. Diomede wounds Venus in *Iliad*, Book 5

317 **Sicani ... Auruncans** early inhabitants of two regions of Italy

396 **Pandarus and Bitias** killed by Turnus at Book 9, lines 750 and 702

405 **Aufidus** Turnus is being sarcastic. Aufidus is a river in Apulia

482 **Tritonian** there was a river Triton in Egypt where Minerva was born

532 **Opis** a nymph of Diana, daughter of Latona. Diana is the goddess of
chastity. She is a vigorous goddess who delights in outdoor pursuits, notably
hunting. Her followers are similarly inclined. Compare the appearance of
Venus as a Spartan huntress who, Aeneas thinks, might be Diana (Book 1,
line 330)

648 **the Amazon Camilla** the Amazons were fierce female warriors who fought
with one breast exposed. They lived in northern Thrace, by the river
Thermodon, in wild and remote country. **Hippolyte** and **Penthesilea** were
famous Amazon leaders. The first married Theseus and the second led the
Amazons to fight for the Trojans (Book 1, line 490)

701 **Ligurians** proverbially liars and deceivers

785 **Soracte** a mountain north of Rome on which a pine fire was built to Apollo,
and through which the worshippers walked three times carrying offerings

BOOK 12   The death of Turnus

A truce is made and broken. Aeneas is wounded. Jupiter forbids Juno to prolong the war any further. Aeneas and Turnus meet in single combat in which Turnus is killed.

In their final rapprochement, Jupiter agrees to Juno's demands: 'Let there be Latium. Let the Alban kings live on from generation to generation and the stock of Rome be made mighty by the manly courage of Italy. Troy has fallen. Let it lie, Troy and the name of Troy' (lines 826–8). The Latins are to prevail in their language, dress and religion. The Trojans are to lose their separate identity and become Latins. The myth of Aeneas proves to be one that expresses the idea of assimilation rather than conquest.

The death of Turnus and the ending of the poem are the subject of Text 3 in Extended Commentaries.

56 **Amata** Turnus's aunt, his mother's sister

83 **Orithyia** wife of Boreas the north wind. Boreas had fathered the royal horses of Troy. Horses are frequently fathered by the various winds, the connection between the two being speed, as here

99 **that effeminate Phrygian** compare the taunts or Iarbas (Book 4, lines 215–17) and Remulus (Book 9, lines 614–20)

146 **Juturna** a daughter of Zeus and nymph of rivers and lakes. There was a lake of Juturna about six miles from the fountain of Numicus

161 **Latinus** according to some accounts a descendant of the sun

347 **Dolon** killed by Diomede (see *Iliad*, Book 10, line 314)

412 **dittany** a herb found on Mount Ida in Crete

701 **Mount Athos, or Mount Eryx or Father Apenninus** mountains in Macedonia, in Sicily and in central Italy respectively

725 **a pair of scales** the destinies of Hector and Achilles are weighed in the scales of Zeus at *Iliad*, Book 20, line 209

766 **Faunus** see Book 7, line 81

845 **Dirae** Tisiphone (see Book 6, lines 555, 557 and Book 10, line 761) and Allecto (see Book 7, line 324) are the twin Dirae, or Furies, together with Megaera. The Dira takes the form of a screech owl, a bird of ill omen

942 **the fatal baldric of the boy Pallas** see Book 10, line 480

PART THREE

CRITICAL APPROACHES

The commentaries following the book by book summaries have pointed to many features of Virgil's art in the management of the plot, the presentation of character, the handling of theme and the use of language. What follows here seeks to give an overall view. This section should be read in conjunction with the account of Virgil's debt to his Roman predecessors that is given in Background.

PLOT: IMITATION OF HOMER

Virgil was not the first Roman poet to make use of the myth of Aeneas (see Background) but he was the first to make it the centre of a whole poem. Like his Roman predecessors he was preoccupied with issues of Roman history and experience but whereas they start with myth and lead up to recent history (their main subject) in a straightforward linear chronological sequence, treating in the process vast stretches of time, Virgil sets his action simply in the mythical world; Roman history is referred to in prophecies of future time. In reverting to the world of myth for the main action, and confining himself to a relatively short period of time, Virgil has followed the example of Homer in giving his **epic** the kind of concentrated **unity of action** that we find in the *Iliad* and *Odyssey* and that was singled out for admiration by the philosopher and critic Aristotle (385–322BC). Virgil's debt to Homer in the conception and making of the *Aeneid* is so central that his handling of the structure and plot can only be appreciated in relation to the epics of his Greek predecessor which it will be necessary to describe in some detail at the outset here.

Aristotle praised Homer because in the *Iliad* the latter did not dramatise the whole of the Trojan story from the beginning to the end but concentrated upon one part, thus having an essential unity while at the same time using many **episodes** to diversify his plot (*Poetics* 23, 5).

Homer's unifying theme is the anger of Achilles. Slighted by Agamemnon, Achilles angrily withdraws from the fighting and cannot be persuaded to return. When the Greeks are in danger of defeat, his friend Patroclus persuades Achilles to allow him to fight wearing his armour. Patroclus is subsequently killed by Hector, the Trojans' champion. Stung by grief and remorse, Achilles returns to the battle to avenge his friend. He kills Hector in single combat and dishonours his corpse by dragging it three times around the tomb of Patroclus. The dreadful consequences of his anger to himself and to others are fully worked out. At the end of the poem Achilles's anger abates somewhat and he agrees to restore Hector's body to Priam for a ransom. All this happens in the course of a few days in the ninth year of the ten-year siege of Troy. At appropriate points Homer fills in the background and makes clear the circumstances of the past which have led to present events. In the speeches of the gods who have knowledge of what is to come and in the fear of mortals, the future is dramatically brought to bear upon the present. Above all there is the doom of Troy destined soon to be razed to the ground. But there is also the doom of Achilles who is to pay for his glory with death, as the dying Hector reminds him in his final words (*Iliad*, Book 22, line 358).

In the case of the *Odyssey*, Aristotle points out that the story itself is quite short and that the poem gains its length from its various episodes (*Poetics* 17, 10). The *Odyssey* is centred upon the return of its hero Odysseus from Troy to Ithaca. The poem opens with a council of the gods in which Athene persuades them to allow her favourite Odysseus, the reluctant prisoner of the nymph Calypso on the island of Ogygia, to return home. Calypso is ordered by Hermes (Mercury) to set Odysseus free. This she does, and he is shipwrecked by Poseidon (Neptune) on the coast of Phaeacia. Here he is well received by Alcinous to whom he tells the story of his ten-year wandering from Troy. He then returns to Ithaca in disguise and restores order in his house by killing the suitors who in his absence have been eating his substance and trying to woo his faithful wife Penelope. The poem ends happily with the reunion of husband and wife and the restoration of order in Ithaca. Again the present action of the *Odyssey* is comparatively short and concentrated. Virgil achieves a similar concentration by starting, like Homer, in the middle of things (*in medias res*), using retrospective narrative for the past and prophecy for future time. In the magnitude of its scope and the variety of its episodes and in its concentration on unity, the *Aeneid* has all the formal characteristics that Aristotle had admired in the Homeric epic.

Virgil's debt to Homer is apparent not only in its Aristotelian structure but also in the content and style of the narrative at every stage. It is a commonplace of later Roman criticism that the first half of the *Aeneid*, taken up substantially with the journey of Aeneas from Troy to Latium, is Virgil's 'Odyssey', while the second half, recounting his battles on arrival, is his 'Iliad'. Virgil's opening invocation recalls Homer's in the *Odyssey*. As Odysseus is helped on his journey from Troy by Athene, so Aeneas is aided by Venus. This divine aid is countered by divine opposition. As Odysseus is pursued across the seas by Poseidon, Aeneas is harried by Juno. At the opening of both epics, the hero has completed most of his journey and recounts his past in an after-dinner speech. The story of the Wooden Horse is Homeric. Aeneas encounters many of the sights and difficulties encountered by Odysseus, and he also speaks to the spirits of the dead.

The second half of Virgil's poem, marked by a second invocation (Book 7, lines 37–45) is the fulfilment of the prophecy which the Sibyl gives to Aeneas: 'I see wars, deadly wars, I see the Thybris foaming with torrents of blood. There you will find a Simois and Xanthus. There, too, will be a Greek camp. A second Achilles is already born in Latium, and he too is the son of a goddess ... Once again the cause of all this Trojan suffering will be a foreign bride, another marriage with a stranger' (Book 6, lines 86–95). Juno is determined to make Aeneas into another Paris who will bring destruction on his people (Book 7, lines 321–2). Paris abducted Helen and thus caused the Trojan War. For Amata, the mother of Lavinia whom Aeneas is to marry, the coming of Aeneas to Latium is an exact parallel to Paris's arrival in Sparta for the purpose of abducting Helen (Book 7, lines 363–5). When the Trojans are besieged in the war, the Italian Remulus calls them bride-stealers and taunts them with shame of being besieged a second time (Book 9, lines 598–601). In some respects the Italian war is a repetition of the Trojan War. In fact, Virgil has reshaped the legends concerning the Trojans in Italy so that his narrative recalls the Trojan War and the Homeric *Iliad* in the outline of its plot, in its incidents and episodes, and in its general style. In other versions of the legend, Aeneas faced opposition lasting a number of years, first from Turnus and after his death from Mezentius. In one version Mezentius killed Aeneas before himself being killed by Ascanius. Virgil has rearranged events, combining all the wars into a single campaign of a few weeks. He makes Mezentius die before Turnus so that Turnus becomes the Trojans' principal antagonist and his death constitutes the climax of the poem. Virgil's war in Italy is more of a systematic campaign than the chaotic fighting in the *Iliad*, but generally speaking the fighting follows the Homeric model of a succession of spectacular incidents involving the prowess and fate of particular heroic figures such as Camilla and Turnus. Moreover, the main lines of the plot specifically recall the *Iliad*. The death of Pallas acts upon Aeneas as the death of Patroclus acts upon Achilles and, like Achilles, Aeneas in anger sacrifices captives to the spirit of his dead friend. In killing Turnus Aeneas avenges the death of Pallas, as Achilles avenges the death of Patroclus in killing Hector.

Other features of the narrative recall Homer. The catalogues of forces in Books 7 and 10 recall Homer's catalogue of ships in Book 2 of the *Iliad*. The funeral games in Book 5 are modelled on Homer's funeral games in Book 23 of the *Iliad*. Venus procures divine armour for her son Aeneas as Thetis has done for Achilles, and in both cases there is an elaborate description of the shield. Most of the epic **similes** in Virgil have their origin in Homer and the gods are called upon to play a similar role. Virgil relied upon Homer to the extent of translating particular passages (compare, for example, the speech of Aeneas at Book 1, lines 198–207 with that of Odysseus in *Odyssey*, Book 12, lines 208–16).

When he composed, the Homeric bard had behind him a continuous tradition refined over several centuries; he was the heir of Demodocus, the resident bard in the king's palace in Phaeacia, who sang from memory with unpremeditated art and immediate inspiration as the god prompted (*Odyssey*, Book 8, lines 44–5; compare Book 22, lines 347–8). For Virgil, who did not work in such a tradition, the writing of heroic poetry was a great labour of reconstruction from a variety of secondary sources, the chief of which was Homer. In his evocation of the mythical world of the past, therefore, Virgil relied substantially upon imitation of his Greek models, chief of which was Homer. The *Aeneid* is, therefore, a monument to the Roman doctrine of creative imitation. That only a great poet could attempt a task of such difficulty with any hope of success is apparent in the reply that Virgil is reported to have made to those critics who accused him of stealing from Homer. He remarked that it is easier to steal Hercules's club than steal one of Homer's verses.

ROMAN THEMES

Virgil has adapted his Greek models to a Roman purpose, and the *Aeneid* is pre-eminently a national **epic** intimately connected with Roman history as well as a record of traditional Roman ways and customs. Virgil's Roman theme is apparent from the start. Aeneas is to found a city which is to be the parent city of Rome (Book 1, lines 7–8). The task is made difficult by the opposition of Juno who harries the Trojans on land and on sea: 'So heavy was the cost of founding the Roman race' (line 33).

In the first of three major prophetic passages which link the mythical world of Aeneas to subsequent Roman history down to Virgil's time, Jupiter unrolls the scroll of fate to reveal the wars to be waged in Italy which are a prelude to everlasting power for the Romans: 'On them I impose no limits of time or place. I have given them an empire that will know no end' (Book 1, lines 278–9). Roman power is therefore divinely supported. Jupiter promises that even Juno will eventually be reconciled to the power of the nation that wears the toga (lines 279–82). This is the civilian dress of the Romans, so that Roman greatness in peace as well as in war is suggested. The celebration of Roman power culminates in a celebration of the **Augustan** peace and the new civil order, **symbolised** by the closing of the gates of the temple of Janus and the restoration of the authority of the old gods of Rome, Fides and Vesta (lines 286–96). (For the significance of these gods see the notes on Book 1.)

The second major prophecy of the Roman future is in Book 6 where Anchises, the proud father, shows Aeneas the roll-call of his Roman descendants (lines 756–886). Romulus appears as the builder of the city who enclosed Rome's seven hills in a single wall (lines 777–84). Next comes Augustus Caesar who will restore the Golden Age to Italy (a mythical time of peace and virtue), and at the same time extend Roman power and influence to the utmost limits of the earth (lines 789–805). Anchises then goes back in time to the heroes of early Rome. As well as those who have served the state in war against the Gauls, there are figures famous in Roman religious and constitutional history, such as

Numa (line 810), the king who is traditionally the founder of the old religion, and Brutus (line 818), Rome's first consul, who expelled the Tarquin kings. Paternal pride in the achievements of the sons of Rome is mingled with paternal sorrow at the prospect of the wounds which the sons of Rome are to inflict upon their fatherland in the civil war of Caesar and Pompey (lines 826–35). The note of pride returns as Anchises then looks to the heroes of foreign conquests over the Greeks and the Carthaginians, at the same time pointing to those noble figures of uncorrupted Roman virtue, whose stern devotion to duty and austere personal integrity later Romans believed was the source of Roman strength and power (lines 836–46). Then comes the proud assertion of the Roman imperial mission (lines 846–53). Others may excel in the arts or in the sciences, but Roman arts are to be the arts of government and rule. The Romans are to subdue the proud but spare the conquered. Roman power is morally justified in the peace that it imposes.

In marked contrast to the philosophic speech of Anchises is the frankly martial spirit of the third major prophecy of Roman power in Book 8, in which Aeneas makes preparations for war. Venus procures arms for her son, and on the great shield, Vulcan, the god of fire, depicts the triumphs of the fearless sons of Mars (lines 625–728). The Romans are descended from Aeneas through Ilia, the mother of Romulus and Remus, but also through Mars, the war god, who is the father of the twins. This ancestry expresses the martial character of the Romans, and the first image on the shield is of the infant sons of the war god, fearlessly being suckled in the cave of Mars by their foster mother, the she-wolf, who fondly licks them into shape (lines 630–4). The ferocity, indeed the rapacity, of the early Romans against their Italian neighbours is apparent in the rape of the Sabine women which follows next (lines 638–8). The god of war is prominent too in the climactic scene at the centre of the shield, in which Augustus leads the Italians into battle at Actium, with the support of the Senate and people of Rome against Mark Antony and Cleopatra with the forces of the East (lines 675–713). In this most nationalistic scene, the gods of Rome assert themselves against the strange deities of the Egyptian East. The Eastern peoples are routed and Cleopatra flees in defeat. Augustus appears not as a civiliser but as the conqueror who triumphantly asserts Roman power. The final image is his Roman triumph in which the conquered peoples of the East are paraded through the streets of Rome (lines 714–28).

Pietas

In Greek legend Aeneas was already famous for his piety. In one version of the events, Aeneas surrendered to the Greeks in the citadel of Troy, and was then allowed safe conduct, in admiration for his piety in choosing to save his father rather than take gold and silver. The image of Aeneas departing from Troy bearing his aged father on his shoulders is found on vases as early as the sixth and fifth centuries BC in Greece and Etruria. His piety (the Latin word is *pietas*) and virtuous reputation were therefore rooted in his dutiful conduct towards his father. Virgil inherits this traditional image, extends it, and makes it central to his poem in a particularly Roman way.

On Troy's last night, Aeneas departs through the flames not only with Anchises on his back but leading his son Ascanius by the hand. Anchises carries with him the images of Troy's gods (Book 2, lines 720–4). Here, concentrated in a single image, is the patriarchal ideal of Roman society: the gods, the fatherland, the grandfather and father, the father and son, the son and grandson, bound to each other in the closest relation, thereby ensuring the survival and the continuous life of the family and the city. This image and all that is contained in it express what *pietas* means for Virgil.

As they flee from Troy, being the able-bodied son who is also a father, Aeneas might be expected to be the central figure, but real authority rests with the elder father Anchises, so that it is Anchises not Aeneas who interprets the omen of the miraculous flame upon the head of Ascanius (Book 2, lines 687–91), which induces him to leave Troy. In their subsequent travels Aeneas defers to Anchises and Anchises interprets the will of the gods. After his death, the spirit of Anchises continues to influence Aeneas through the medium of dreams. At Carthage this influence reinforces the order of Jupiter that Aeneas must leave Dido because he is neglecting his mission, thereby cheating Ascanius of his inheritance (Book 4, lines 351–3). Aeneas promptly leaves, and is driven by a storm to Sicily – '... do not believe this is without the will of the gods' (Book 5, line 56) – where he reverently invokes the spirit of Anchises on the anniversary of his death and offers libations and sacrifices at his tomb (lines 77–103). The ceremonies and rites there performed are exactly those of the Roman family festival called the *Parentalia* held annually in February, at which the head of the family, the *paterfamilias*, made offerings to the spirits of the dead. The spirit of Anchises responds with a favourable manifestation in the form of a snake (lines 84–93). Aeneas then institutes funeral games in his father's honour, in the course of which he is himself seen effectively in the role of father (and called the son of Anchises at line 244), as he benevolently presides over the games and over the youthful equestrian pageant led by his son Ascanius. The three generations of the Trojan line are now in harmonious relation after the disturbance of Carthage. When the women burn the ships, Aeneas falters, but he is reassured by the spirit of his father in a dream, in which Anchises directs Aeneas to continue his journey to Italy and to visit him by descending into Hades (Book 5, lines 725–39). Aeneas is obediently acquiescent to his father's will. In welcoming him there, Anchises commends him for his piety in making such a difficult journey and expresses the fear he had felt that some harm would come to him at Carthage (Book 6, lines 687–94). Aeneas replies that the gloomy image of his father often coming to him had compelled him to make the journey (lines 695–6). Anchises first shows Aeneas his Trojan ancestors and then his Roman descendants whom he fondly regards as his 'sons' (line 832). After communion with his father in Hades, Aeneas confidently interprets omens and signs from the gods (Book 7, lines 116–34). Where he had taken upon his shoulders the burden of the past at Troy, he now lifts upon his shoulders the shield given to him by his mother on which are engraved the fame and fortunes of his Roman descendants (Book 8, line 731). He holds the shield as he stands before the altar to offer prayer and sacrifice before the final combat. Here he is described as 'Father Aeneas, the founder of the Roman race' (Book 12, line 166). Ascanius 'the second hope for the future greatness of Rome' is at his side (line 168). To Ascanius he sets himself as an example to be followed (lines 435–40). He is now himself a true father.

The relationship between father and son is the closest bond in the poem. The strength of this bond is variously reflected in different emotions at critical moments in the main action of the last three books.

As at Troy, Aeneas's first thoughts after witnessing the slaughter of Priam had been for his own father (Book 2, lines 559–62), so in the war in Italy, after killing Lausus who had vainly attempted to rescue his father Mezentius, the son of Anchises (so called at Book 10, line 822) sees in the brave sacrifice of the young Lausus a reflection of his own filial piety (Book 10, line 824). Similarly, the worst an enemy can do is to violate this relationship. Pyrrhus takes an unholy delight in killing one of Priam's sons before his eyes (Book 2, lines 526–53), and Turnus when facing Pallas (whom Virgil has made the son rather than the grandson of Evander) wishes that Evander could be present to watch (Book 10, line 443). Later, taught humility by the fortunes of war, Turnus begs Aeneas in the name of Anchises to pity his own father Daunus and spare his life (Book 12, lines 932–6).

This bond between father and son is consummated in the meeting between Aeneas and Anchises in Hades. The descent into the underworld is an expression of that reverence for the ancestors which was a dominant feature of the traditional Roman religion, and it is also an acknowledgement of the power of the father, *patria potestas*, which in early Rome had been absolute. Later in the poem, Virgil prophesies that his poetry will be immortal 'while the house of Aeneas remains by the immovable rock of the Capitol and the Father of the Romans still keeps his empire' (Book 9, lines 448–9). The state, whether it be the Republic which was ruled by the patrician fathers of the Senate (the *patres conscripti*) or – as translated here – the Empire, ruled by a single father (Augustus was saluted by the Senate as '*pater patriae*' in 2BC) is therefore seen to be an extension of the family in which the father reigned supreme.

CHARACTER

AENEAS

Granted his role in the poem as the chosen instrument of the gods and the part he must play in the grand patriarchal design, it is not surprising that 'pious' Aeneas emerges as little more than a **symbol**, passively acquiescent towards the will of the gods or of his father. What is perhaps surprising is that Aeneas nowhere shows any relish for the great enterprise in which he is engaged, nor does he himself display much enterprise or positive will in carrying out his task. In this he is to be sharply distinguished from the stern examples of Roman gravity admired by Anchises, on which Virgil might have chosen to model him. Nor does he show much of the fighting spirit celebrated by Vulcan on the shield. In fact, far from being like the stern and hardened Romans or the efficient and decisive Caesars who are his Roman descendants, Trojan Aeneas in the early stages of his journey displays the psychology of a defeated exile and victim of traumatic misfortune. As a wandering Trojan who has lost his home and city, he is uncertain of himself, susceptible to sudden feelings of terror and frequently prone to tears. At the opening of the poem, in a fit of fright and despair after the storm, he envies those who had died before their fathers at Troy (Book 1, lines 92–101), and he weeps copiously upon seeing the sufferings of the Trojans depicted in the temple of Juno at Carthage (Book 1, lines 464–5).

This characterisation of Aeneas is apparent in Virgil's version of the part played by him in the fall of Troy. In one version of the story Aeneas had been warned by the gods in advance and left before the incident of the Wooden Horse. Virgil of course needed Aeneas as a witness to the fall with which he is strongly identified. In another version Aeneas so successfully resisted the Greeks that he was able to negotiate his withdrawal from a position of strength upon the citadel of Troy. Virgil could therefore have cast Aeneas in the role of hero, but his Aeneas is neither resourceful nor successful. He joins in the slaughter in defence of Troy when he falls in with someone else's plan to put on the armour of dead Greeks and so confuse the enemy (Book 2, lines 386–401). But this Trojan plan to meet trickery with trickery goes badly wrong when their own side starts killing them in error (lines 410–12), and resistance proves futile (line 402). Aeneas escapes with the aid of Venus (Book 2, line 632), who prevents him from wasting time in taking revenge on Helen, an act which he himself recognises as inglorious (Book 2, line 584). As he tells his tale he recoils from the horror of it (Book 2, lines 2–12). As he sees it, the destruction of Troy is achieved through deception, barbarously executed and above all unmerited (Book 3, lines 1–2).

After the fall of Troy, the 'Odyssey' of Aeneas is conceived in a spirit wholly different from the *Odyssey* of Homer. Aeneas shows none of the zest for adventure or resourcefulness associated with the Homeric

Odysseus. In the episode which is most Homeric, the encounter with the Harpies (Book 3, lines 209–79), Aeneas's resistance is as futile as the resistance he offers to the insubstantial monsters of Hades (Book 6, lines 291–4), and the Trojans flee dejected and fearful as they had fled from Thrace where Polydorus met his grisly end (Book 3, lines 60–2), and as they flee from Sicily pursued by the monstrous Cyclopes (lines 655–6). Where Odysseus had wittily risen to the challenge of the Cyclops (*Odyssey*, Book 9, lines 105–566), Aeneas listens to the horror story of one of the companions of Odysseus who had been left behind in the Cyclops's den (Book 3, lines 588–654). Typically, Aeneas is cast in the role of listener in his wanderings as he had been a witness of Troy's downfall. He hears prophecies of future difficulties and tales of past horror. When he meets Andromache he envies those who have built their walls and do not have to chase a fugitive destiny across the seas (lines 493–7).

At Carthage he finds shelter and relief from misery until he is struck dumb with fear by the intervention of Jupiter (Book 4, lines 279–80) and terrified by the spirit of his father in dreams (Book 4, lines 351–3). He assures Dido that he does not seek Italy willingly (line 361), telling her that if he were a free agent he would return to rebuild Troy (lines 341–4). In Sicily, he contemplates giving up his journey when the Trojan women burn the ships (Book 5, lines 700–4). For Aeneas, the destined journey only serves to add loss on to loss, and there are recurring images of his personal unhappiness, reflecting an inner loneliness and a restless longing for comfort and security. When his mother Venus departs from him in her disguise as a Carthaginian huntress, Aeneas reproaches her for avoiding direct conversation and embrace (Book 1, lines 407–9). He vainly tries to embrace the spirit of Creusa at Troy (Book 2, lines 792–4), and the spirit of his father both when he sees him in the dream in Sicily (Book 5, lines 741–2) and when they meet in Hades (Book 6, lines 700–2).

In Hades, although he had assured the Sibyl beforehand that no form of suffering was unknown to him (Book 6, lines 103–5), he relives the horrors and sorrows of the past in a new form, learning of the fates of Palinurus (lines 337–83), Dido (lines 450–76) and Deiphobus (lines 494–547). He greets Anchises with pleasure in Elysium (lines 695–702), but when Anchises explains to him the doctrine of the transmigration of souls and shows him the spirits awaiting a new earthly life, he wonders what dread desire impels them to the light of earth (line 721). Finally, there is no comment from Aeneas on the roll-call of Roman heroes; the enthusiasm is all from Anchises.

There is little essential change in Aeneas after the revelation of the future in Hades. Although he is firmer of purpose in that there are no backward glances towards Troy, Aeneas does not emerge as a man who acts from controlled strength derived from special interior knowledge. Relief at the longed-for arrival at their destination in Italy soon gives way to familiar anxiety, and the prospect of war brings with it gloom and depression (Book 8, lines 18–30). At Pallanteum there is momentary relief, even pleasure, but here Aeneas is once again cast primarily in the role of listener and spectator. When he dutifully raises the shield upon his shoulder Virgil detaches the hero from the scenes depicted upon it with the remark that Aeneas took pleasure in the representation of events of which he was unaware (line 730). Evander welcomes him but he is a stranger in a foreign land and his enemies are quick to mock his effeminate appearance and dress (Book 12, lines 95–100).

In the course of the war, like the rest of the participants, he is carried away by the emotions it releases and in a fit of terrible anger when Turnus kills Pallas he loses all self-control. The momentary pleasure he had experienced at Pallanteum intensifies his pain as he feels acutely the loss of friendship and warm fellowship that had eluded him since the fall of Troy (Book 10, lines 515–17). With Troy he loses his home and Creusa his wife (Book 2, lines 738–95). On his journey he loses his father (Book 3, lines 709–15), then he is forced to give up Dido. To the loss of most of what is closest to him are added the losses of his friends: Hector, Orontes, Palinurus and Misenus, and now Pallas and what Pallas represents. Where previously he had shed tears, he now shows unwonted anger and commits acts of barbarism and savagery alien to his better self, beginning with the sacrifice of eight captive youths to the spirit of Pallas (Book 10, lines 517–20), in the manner of Achilles who had similarly sacrificed captives to the spirit of Patroclus (*Iliad*, Book 22, lines 27–8). However, unlike the Homeric Achilles Aeneas is not a natural warrior who finds the battlefield a stage upon which he can excel and achieve fame and glory. As he formally bids farewell to Pallas on his last journey back to Evander, Aeneas sees the war as a grim manifestation of destiny involving sorrow and misery (Book 11, lines 96–8). As the moment for the last combat arrives Aeneas is eager for the conclusion (Book 12, line 430), but in his departing words to his son he moralises upon his own misfortune (lines 435–40). In the final moment as the defeated Turnus is begging for mercy, Aeneas catches sight of the belt of Pallas (lines 941–5) and the anger caused by the pain of loss returns. The killing of Turnus answers Evander's prayer for vengeance (Book 11, lines 176–81), but in Virgil's presentation is rather the fulfilment of anger than a pious duty performed, so that the poem ends neither with the magnanimous exercise of Roman power envisaged by Anchises, nor with the triumphant assertion of Roman power depicted upon the shield, but **ironically** with Aeneas for the first time having his heart truly in his task and truly the victim of his own grim destiny.

D IDO

Dido is a strong woman and is perhaps the most strongly drawn of all Virgil's characters. The poem's first readers in the light of recent history might have expected the queen with whom Aeneas lingers at Carthage to resemble the historical Cleopatra with whom Mark Antony dallied in Egypt (see Background) but Dido is nothing like the sensual figure of Oriental mystery made famous in Shakespeare's characterisation of her in his play *Antony and Cleopatra* (1609). Nor is she like the character Calypso in Homer's *Odyssey*, a goddess who constrains the hero against his will. In the larger historical **allegory**, in the person of Dido is prefigured the opposition to Roman power presented by Carthage, but although she proves to be passionate she is far from being the embodiment of a Roman idea of Carthaginian ferocity.

   Before she appears, there is a sympathetic account of her when Venus tells Aeneas of her great love for her first husband Sychaeus and her flight from Tyre after his murder at the hands of her brother Pygmalion (lines 339–70). Dido, like Aeneas an exile and a fugitive victim of treachery, is sympathetically presented from the beginning. She is a sensitive and humane ruler who comes from a civilisation comparable in its wealth and art to Troy, and who is building a city that is all that

Aeneas could wish his own to be. In the temple of Juno in which Dido (who does not worship strange gods) is first encountered at the beginning of the poem, the queen as lawgiver (lines 507–8), dispenses justice, and the Trojans appeal to her as to one who has a civilising mission (lines 522–3). The setting reinforces a sympathetic view of Dido as a compassionate ruler who welcomes the Trojans unconditionally without being cajoled into such a welcome by divine intervention (lines 628–30). The mean trick whereby through the joint plan of Juno and Venus (who have their own motives) she is later beguiled into falling in love with Aeneas intensifies sympathy for her and casts her in the role of the plaything of higher powers.

Dido's love for Aeneas is referred to as a *culpa* (Book 4, line 172), a matter for blame, and she may be seen as a warning example of what happens when a person gives way to passion, but nevertheless she is not presented as an immoral woman. She hesitates and consults her sister before giving rein to her feelings. When Aeneas is terrified into leaving, Virgil's focus is upon Dido's reactions and feelings which are sympathetically represented. Furthermore, Virgil allows her to speak with a passionate eloquence that contrasts markedly with Aeneas's tight-lipped evasions. His argument that if the fates allowed he would rather go back to Troy, for their lies his love, is insensitive to say the least and provokes what seems like an entirely justifiable response.

Dido is overwhelmed by his ingratitude, by the heartlessness of his farewell speech to her and by the injustice of it all, scorning the notion that the gods could possibly support such behaviour (lines 365–80). Although she appeals to him, she does not try to constrain him and the magic to which she resorts is a disguise under the cover of which she plans suicide. Her suicide is prompted by feelings not only of betrayal but also of self-betrayal. After Aeneas's desertion her political position is undermined, and pride, apart from practical difficulties, prevents her from following him (lines 534–46). But, above all, she has lost her self-respect. She regrets that she is unable to live the unconscious life of a wild beast that has no moral awareness of its own behaviour, and as Aeneas is haunted by the spirit of Anchises, she is haunted by the memory of her dead husband Sychaeus whose love she has betrayed (lines 550–3). Her cult of Sychaeus, which is comparable to Andromache's cult of Hector (Book 3, lines 303–5), caused her scruples as she began to feel love for Aeneas (Book 4, lines 20–9) and shows her to be a character of special moral sensitivity.

With the realisation that she has betrayed her moral being to no effect, Dido is dishonoured in her own eyes and loses the will to live. As she watches the fleet depart, her passion is vented in hatred of Aeneas (lines 590–629). For Dido, his desertion shows Aeneas's essential nature, whatever others may say of the man who carried his country's gods from Troy with his father on his shoulders. She wishes she had torn him limb from limb, or served up Ascanius to him to feast upon and so extinguished the whole race with father and son. Finally she curses Aeneas, wishing him every misfortune and hoping that he will be torn from Ascanius and meet an early death. It is the psychologically credible reaction of a strongly passionate nature, continued after death when her spirit resolutely refuses to respond to Aeneas in Hades (Book 6, lines 469–74).

DIDO & AENEAS

The sacrifice of the individual to the fates that led inexorably to the foundation of Rome is most intensely dramatised in the encounter of Aeneas with Dido at Carthage, and it is further confirmed when Aeneas meets Dido in Hades. Here Aeneas's individual will is wholly subdued, and Dido is the innocent victim of the Roman destiny.

When she enters the temple of Juno Dido is likened to the goddess Diana leading her dancers on Delos (Book 1, lines 496–504). Later, after Dido has fallen in love with him, when he is arriving for the hunting party Aeneas is likened in appearance and beauty to Apollo (Book 4, lines 142–50). With the Apollo **simile** the identification of Aeneas with Dido reaches its culmination. In their god-like beauty and grace, in their dignity and bearing, and in the high estimation in which they are held by others, Aeneas and Dido, like Apollo and Diana, are twin brother and sister. Furthermore, in their aesthetic awareness and their civilised enjoyments, in their sensitivity to suffering resulting from comparable past misfortunes and in their harsh destinies as leaders of exiled peoples through danger and difficulty, Aeneas and Dido seem deliberately designed by Virgil to be complementary reflections of one another.

We have no direct insight into the feelings of Aeneas for Dido, but, whatever the public status of their relationship about which they later disagree, Virgil makes it clear that the consummation of their love in the cave (lines 160–8) is a union upon which nature looks kindly and not the squalid affair that rumour makes of it later (lines 173–97). However, the Roman destiny intervenes in the form of a message from Jupiter (lines 265–76), and patriarchal values are asserted to the exclusion of Dido.

As the destruction of Dido by Aeneas is enacted **symbolically** in her falling upon his sword, so the ritual burning of the portrait and the belongings of Aeneas upon the funeral pyre together with their marriage bed is a most powerful symbol not only of Dido's love turned to hatred but also of Aeneas's self-immolation and sacrifice at Carthage. In leaving Dido, Aeneas loses himself, though he is never fully aware of this loss, and, ignorant of what has happened, he sails away to Sicily where he invokes his father's spirit, and thence to the underworld where he consummates his sacrifice. Aeneas is not a vital character like the heroes of Homer, because all his vital instincts and passions are subdued in the service of the patriarchal ideal. However, denial of love and sacrifice of self beget tears, frustration and anger so that in a symbolic sense Dido's curse comes true.

The Dido episode is, therefore, fully integrated into the design of the *Aeneid;* it is the place in the poem where the sacrifice imposed by the Roman patriarchal state is most apparent in the protest of the sacrificial female victim. The protest also occurs in minor incidents such as the burning of the ships by the Trojan women (Book 5, lines 604–99) or the lament of the mother of Euryalus (Book 9, lines 481–97). In the Dido episode, the sacrifice is not presented as a noble one; it is brought about by fear and results in self-destruction and calamity for the innocent with terrible future consequences. As Aeneas is linked to Rome, so Dido is linked to Carthage. In cursing Aeneas, Dido hopes for everlasting hatred between the two nations with the coming of an avenger who will pursue the descendants of Troy (Book 4, lines 621–9). Her prophecy bears fruit in the career of Hannibal, but the greater prophecy is foreshadowed in Dido's own fate, the future doom of Carthage itself, razed to the ground by the Romans in 146BC. In pronouncing her own epitaph (lines 651–8), Dido hails her achievements in founding a great city, calling herself fortunate if only the Trojan ships had not touched the Carthaginian shore. When rumour of her death goes round the city, the women wail as if Carthage, like Troy before it, was falling before the invading enemy and being consumed by fire (lines 666–71). Once again Virgil's sympathy is all with the defeated, and this time obliquely with the victims of Roman power.

TURNUS

When Aeneas seeks prophecies from the Sibyl at Cumae, she tells him that she sees the river Tiber foaming with torrents of blood; she continues: 'A second Achilles is already born in Latium, and he too is the son of a goddess' (Book 6, line 89). She is referring to Turnus, the son of Venilia a sea nymph, the leader of the Rutulians who is also a suitor for the hand of Lavinia, the daughter of Latinus. Like Dido, therefore, he stands in the way of the Roman destiny and resists the settlement of Aeneas that is welcomed by Latinus. Although the parallel with Achilles may suggest a ruthless implacable ferocity, he is, like Dido, not unsympathetically represented. He is a figure of undoubted courage who is prepared to fight for his cause, and may be regarded as a worthy representative of the kind of Italian strength on which the future power of the Roman state is to depend (Book 12, line 827). Sympathy is created for him by the way in which he is seen to be the plaything of the Fury Allecto as she inflames him to war by hurling a burning torch at his breast (Book 7, lines 456ff.). His personal integrity is clear in the contrast with Drances in the council (Book 11). It is often said that he is a kind of foil to Aeneas, representing an older individual heroism typified in the character to which he has been compared in the poem itself, the Homeric Achilles. His death at the hands of Aeneas at the end of the poem is not the occasion of any Trojan triumph but is so narrated as to evoke sympathy for the defeated, those who are the victims of the Roman destiny (see Extended Commentaries, Text 3).

THE ROLE OF THE GODS OR DIVINE MACHINERY

Virgil's vision of the world is apparent in the uses to which he puts his **'divine machinery'** of anthropomorphic deities which he adapted from

Homer. In the Dido **episode** Jupiter and Juno are only concerned with their grander purposes, to which the human individual is readily sacrificed without a qualm. Jupiter, when dealing with Aeneas, proves a very stern heavenly version of the Roman father. Juno willingly acquiesces in the mean trick instigated by Venus, whereby Dido falls in love with Aeneas, while Venus shows little regard for the personal happiness of her son at Carthage.

Furthermore, the efforts Venus makes to protect her son elsewhere in the poem serve to emphasise the fact that Aeneas survives not by his own will and enterprise but because he is the chosen instrument of the divine will. Yet there is no single divine will, since each of the gods has his or her own individual will which may conflict with that of another and may be exercised blindly in ignorance of the Fates. Jupiter is confident in his knowledge of the Fates when he grandly surveys the future from the viewpoint of eternity at the beginning of the poem (Book 1, lines 227–96) but later is baffled by the turn of events, saying that he has forbidden the war in Latium (Book 10, line 8). He withdraws, letting the Fates find their own way (lines 104–13). Only in the final moment does he forbid Juno to pursue her opposition further and then, admitting defeat, he yields to her plea that the Trojans should lose their identity in Latium (Book 12, lines 791–842). Jupiter's will is modified by the actions of Juno with whom he is constantly at cross purposes and with whom he must compromise. After the compromise, divine support for the opposition to Aeneas is withdrawn and the Fates find their way, but not before Jupiter has sent a horrid Fury to terrify Turnus (Book 12, lines 843–68). Though the gods play a part in the final combat between Achilles and Hector, there is no equivalent in Homer of this ugly manifestation of the malignant power of fate. But it is the key to Virgil's presentation of the death of Turnus. In the final moments all attention is directed to his fearful agony and all sympathy felt for him as the victim of inexorable fate. To Aeneas's final taunt, he replies that no words of Aeneas can frighten him. It is the gods and the hostility of Jupiter that terrify him (Book 12, lines 894–5). Where previously, as the victim of fate, Aeneas had been full of pity, as the agent of fate he is pitiless. Nor is any moral superiority that Aeneas may have over Turnus apparent in the fatal victory, the power of fate being indifferent to individual moral and human concerns.

Once the Romans had arrived at world dominion, their steady rise to power doubtless looked inevitable, and long before Virgil they had attributed it to divine providence. Delivering his opening prophecy Jupiter is benign, dignified and confident as he takes a long view and looks forward to the Roman peace. However, Virgil takes no comfortable view of his nation's history. Aeneas has reason to quake at the terror of Jupiter's will in Carthage and Turnus experiences the full terror of Jupiter's power in Latium. Juno, who opposes the Roman destiny and unleashes all that is subdued and repressed in the grand patriarchal design, is finally forced to yield to the superior power of her husband. But anger lives on in the human sphere (Book 12, line 946). Jupiter and his sister Juno contribute more or less equally to the anger and terror with which the poem ends. The gods therefore represent conflicting forces through which the fates find their way. A particular god may seem benign, or, if hostile, may be appeased for a time, but there is no escape from fate itself.

THE FATAL VISION

The *Aeneid* is a most fatalistic poem and Virgil's melancholy fatalism underlies the narrative at every turn. When Hector's spirit visits Aeneas in a dream on Troy's fatal night (Book 2, lines 267–97), Aeneas hails Hector, in spite of his mangled appearance, as the surest hope of Troy and asks him why he has delayed his return for so long. Hector does not stop to answer Aeneas's vain question, but tells him to leave the city straightaway as the enemy is within. Aeneas does not follow Hector's direction immediately but offers resistance that proves futile.

The **episode** is a dramatisation of the **irony** of human hope, and of mortal ignorance of the unforeseen and mortal impotence in the face of the inevitable. The overwhelming power of remorseless fate is most clearly apparent in the events that lead to the destruction of Troy when Venus reveals to Aeneas what would normally be hidden from mortal sight, a vision of the gods energetically engaged in knocking down the walls of Troy (Book 2, lines 604–23). In the face of such indomitable power, Aeneas submits to the inevitable and withdraws to make good his escape. Apparent here is the larger vision of things underlying the main action. Aeneas can only submit to fate and the will of the gods, hoping to escape trials and tribulations by being forewarned, and finally enduring what cannot be avoided. In his wanderings, the prophet Helenus tells Aeneas how to avoid Scylla and Charybdis (Book 3, lines 415–32) and, with the help of Anchises, Aeneas manages to do so (lines 558–67). Helenus also advises Aeneas to visit the Sibyl who will tell him about the wars in Italy and how he is to avoid or endure each toil (lines 441–62). Later in Sicily, when Aeneas despairs after the burning of the ships by the women and contemplates giving up his journey, a Trojan elder urges the necessity of following wherever the Fates may lead in their erratic path, for every eventuality can be overcome through endurance (Book 5, lines 700–10). In Hades Anchises (not the Sibyl) tells Aeneas how he is to endure or avoid each toil (Book 6, lines 890–92). Unfortunately in the second half of the poem Aeneas is not very successful either in avoiding the unbearable or in bearing the unavoidable.

Virgil's philosophy of life is expressed in his conception of Hades. In Homer, the spirit of Achilles, who in his life on earth had chosen a short life with glory in preference to a long life without distinction, comes to Odysseus from Hades and tells him that he would rather be the meanest slave on earth than rule the kingdom of the dead (*Odyssey*, Book 11, lines 465–86). Homer makes us feel the preciousness of earthly life when we compare it with the **pathos** of the continuing consciousness of disembodied spirits in the twilight kingdom of death. For Virgil there is no such obvious comparison, and his Hades is the product of his sense of the horror of existence while at the same time it offers the consolations of philosophy. The hope of something better in the world beyond is represented by the presence of the spirit of Anchises amongst the spirits of the blessed in Elysium. The good are rewarded if not in life then in the afterlife. Here in the spirit world Aeneas meets his father in a secluded valley where the spirits who are fated to be reincarnated are about to drink the waters of Lethe, thereby forgetting their former life (Book 6, lines 703–18). Aeneas finds it difficult to believe that ethereal spirits revert to the sluggish bodies and asks what is the meaning of their dread desire for earthly existence (lines 719–21). Anchises then unfolds the mysteries of the purification of the spirit from the body's taint and the doctrine of the reincarnation of the soul (lines 722–51). Like Aeneas, he regards the body as the spirit's enemy, affirming the Platonic idea that the body is the prison of the soul while emotions are the perturbation of the spirit. Fears and desires, joys and sorrows alike disturb the soul's tranquillity. Anchises does not draw any conclusions from this, since his aim is simply to explain to Aeneas the doctrine of reincarnation and to show him his Roman descendants. But according to this philosophy, earthly life is largely a snare and a delusion. Certainly the emotions originating in the body are invariably a snare and a source of human misery in the *Aeneid*. Sexual passion in Dido is conceived as a maddening invasion by a hostile power. Her love is a wound (Book 4, lines 1–2), and she is likened to a stricken deer (lines 68–73). To Virgil, to feel strong emotion is to lose control and be carried away. Dido raves like a Bacchanal (lines 300–3); Amata and the Latin women are similarly possessed (Book 7, lines 385–405). If the emotions are a snare, then human aspirations and desires are invariably a delusion. Troy in its fall becomes a **symbol** of the emptiness of human pride and the vanity of human wishes. 'Dread desire' is almost a recurring formula. Eagerly volunteering for the adventure in which he is to die Nisus asks whether the gods are responsible for such enthusiasm or whether each man makes his own dread desire a god (Book 9, lines 184–5). He and Euryalus, who shows all the courage of inexperienced youth until he loses his way and is deluded by his own fears (line 305), are victims of their own dread desire for slaughter and plunder. Camilla is the most energetic physical force in the poem but she is carried away in the fighting by her vain desire to possess as a spoil of war the gold armour of her Phrygian foe, and so becomes blind to all danger (Book 11, lines 778–82). Turnus revels in his own strength and prowess, eagerly joining battle like a stallion who has broken free from his tether (Book 11, lines 484–97), but at the end of the poem, as he staggers beneath the weight of a stone which proves too heavy for him to throw, he is deluded in his faith in his physical powers and likened to one in a nightmare who finds himself unable to act, a powerful image of the body's paralysis (Book12, lines 901–12). Virgil shares Anchises's mistrust of the body and his recoil from the passions. Underlying the narrative is a strong sense of the futility of human action and the insubstantiality of earthly life.

What follow here are hints for the reader who knows no Latin. The general pitch of Virgil's style is well illustrated in the opening lines of Dryden's famous translation (1697), called by his fellow poet Alexander Pope the most noble and spirited in the English language: even though he uses the rhyming **decasyllabic** couplet (Virgil's **hexameters** do not use rhyme), his verse paragraphs capture the heroic note better than any other version in English.

> Arms, and the Man I sing, who, forc'd by Fate,
> And haughty Juno's unrelenting Hate;
> Expell'd and exil'd, left the Trojan shoar:
> Long Labours, both by Sea and Land, he bore;
> And in the doubtful War, before he won
> The Latian Realm, and built the destin'd Town:
> His banish'd Gods restor'd to Rites Divine,
> And setl'd sure Succession in his Line:
> From whence the Race of Alban Fathers come,
> And the long Glories of Majestick Rome.

Virgil is here announcing his grand theme, and the style of Dryden is appropriately grand. The heroic note is immediately apparent in the rhythm and arrangement of the opening words 'Arms, and the Man I sing', and the elevated and serious tone is sustained throughout the passage. The majestic sweep of the final line is a fitting climax to the grand opening, expressing in its rhythm, its sound and its movement the theme with which the opening culminates, the majesty and grandeur of Rome. When he began translating Virgil Dryden wrote in the preface to his *Sylvae* 'I looked on Virgil as a succinct and grave majestic writer ... His verse is everywhere sounding the very thing in your ears whose sense it bears'. All readers of Virgil recognise the truth of this, and Dryden has endeavoured to produce an equivalent style in English. Here is another short passage where the souls of the blessed in Elysium are compared to bees:

> About the Boughs an Airy Nation flew,
> Thick as the humming Bees, that hunt the golden Dew;
> In Summer's heat, on tops of Lillies feed,
> And creep within their Bells, to suck the balmy Seed.

The winged Army roams the Field around;

The Rivers and the Rocks remurmur to the sound.

(Virgil, Book 6, lines 706–9; Dryden, Book 6, lines 958–63)

Dryden here provides an equivalent for the highly figured style of Virgil. The souls are described **figuratively** in the dignified **periphrasis** of 'airy nation', and then figuratively again in the second periphrasis with a military **metaphor** as a 'winged Army'. There is a discreet **hyperbole** in the rivers and the rocks remurmuring to the sound. Such use of figures has the effect of elevating the language beyond the commonplace. The sweet humming of the bees is well suggested in the various patterns of sound created by the repetition of consonants and by the skilful interplay of vowel sounds within and between lines. This use of **alliteration** and **assonance** is not obtrusive as particular sound effects are subordinated to the overall music and movement of the verse. Within the pattern of smooth, flowing regularity with which the passage opens and with which it is elegantly concluded, there is sufficient variation in the rhythm, with pauses at different places in the lines, to suggest the activity of the bees. In fact, the organisation of sound and movement gives emphasis to the visual image of the bees' activity among the lilies which is most sensuously conveyed. There is a harmony of sound and sense, as well as a metrical and musical harmony, as we see and hear the bees. Accordingly, the art is not an end in itself but the means by which the image is made fully natural.

Dryden wrote in the preface to his translation that Virgil 'is everywhere elegant sweet and flowing in his hexameters'. He aims to be similar in his heroic couplets. His language is artfully arranged, and the art is unmistakably directed towards elegance and harmony. In this he is a disciple of Virgil, as he is in the belief he expresses in the preface to his translation that in an heroic poem even the least parts should be 'grave, majestical and sublime'. In translating Virgil Dryden aimed for a consistently serious and elevated style. This he achieves both by the management of metre and sound, and by the use of **rhetorical** figures which raise the language above the everyday and the familiar. But while he follows Virgil in his use of figures, the actual words he uses, generally speaking, are not a special vocabulary invented for poetry or reserved for a high style. In the two extracts discussed there is not a single word that could not readily be used in prose. The words are common enough, and concrete and physical in their reference. Similarly, Virgil for the most part uses the vocabulary of prose. Of Dryden's language it has been said by the nineteenth-century English poet Gerard Manley Hopkins that it represents 'the native thew and sinew of the English language' ('thew' means 'muscle'). This is a source of the strength and vigour of his translation of Virgil, which, despite any faults it might have, remains the best version of Virgil in English and the best guide for the reader without Latin to the general features of the Virgilian **epic** and its narrative style. Here is a third passage illustrating what Pope called Dryden's 'energy divine':

> So stoops the yellow Eagle from on high,
> And bears a speckled Serpent thro' the Sky;
> Fast'ning his crooked Tallons on the Prey:
> The Pris'ner hisses thro' the liquid Way,
> Resists the Royal Hawk, and, tho' opprest,
> She fights in Volumes, and erects her Crest:
> Turn'd to her Foe, she stiffens ev'ry Scale;
> And shoots her forky Tongue, and whisks her threat'ning Tail.
> Against the Victour, all Defence is weak:
> The imperial Bird still plies her with his Beak;
> He tears her Bowels, and her Breast he gores;
> Then claps his Pinions, and securely soars.
> (Virgil, Book 11, lines 751–6; Dryden, Book 11, lines 1105–16)

After he had completed his Virgil Dryden expressed the hope in his preface that he had managed to copy 'the clearness, the purity, the easiness, and the magnificence of his style'.

THE SIMILES

A notable feature of Virgil's narrative is his use of the formal **simile** which is a traditional component of the **epic** style. Virgil's similes are carefully integrated into the surrounding narrative, and like other kinds of imagery are rich in implication, suggestion and association. For example, when Aeneas steps out of the cloud to be revealed to Dido he shines like a god, for Venus had enhanced his beauty:

THE SIMILES continued

> Like polish'd Iv'ry, beauteous to behold,
>
> Or Parian Marble, when enchas'd in Gold,
>
> (Virgil, Book 1, lines 586–93; Dryden, Book 1, lines 830–1)

The emphasis upon the physical beauty of Aeneas, which is intensified by the simile, is appropriate, given that Dido is to fall in love with Aeneas. But the simile also reflects the impression of material beauty, opulence and cultivated splendour with which Virgil wishes us to associate Carthage. The ivory, the marble and the gold are in keeping with the general imagery of the latter half of the first book, and accordingly there is the implication that Aeneas himself is not out of place in this setting.

The more extended similes of which there are many in the poem are elaborate images that can be intricately connected with the main narrative. For example, when Dido has fallen in love with Aeneas she is likened in her restless wandering to a deer which has been caught unawares and hit unwittingly by the arrow of a shepherd; the deer flees with the deadly arrow in her side (Book 4, lines 68–73). The simile expresses the classical conception of love as an overwhelming destructive force that brings pain and ruin to those who are afflicted by it. Not only is the deer doomed but the shepherd does not even know that he has hit her, as of course Aeneas does not realise what is happening either when Dido falls in love with him or later when he fails to recognise his part in her undoing. Apart from restless movement which is the immediate point of the comparison, Dido's pain, her inability to do anything about it, and her ultimate destruction are all prefigured in the simile. Her predicament is vividly summed up in this arresting image which evokes sympathy for her as the innocent victim, and illustrates the nature and predicts the outcome of her love affair with Aeneas.

Similes are, therefore, key pointers to the significance of what is happening in the larger narrative in which they occur. In the account of the fall of Troy in Book 2, the similes, all comprising natural imagery, reflect the viewpoint of Aeneas and the emotions aroused in him by the fall of Troy as he tells the tale. Laocoon, as he is being strangled by the monstrous snakes that have come from the sea, issues cries like the bellowings of a wounded bull that has escaped from a sacrifice (lines 223–4). The simile intensifies the horror and evokes sympathy for the innocent Laocoon. As Aeneas sees from the rooftop of his father's house the invading Greeks setting fire to Troy, it is as if fire is seizing the cornfields, or a raging torrent is bearing away the crops and destroying the farmer's labours while a shepherd looks on bewildered from the safety of a rock above the scene (lines 304–9). In this simile human endeavour is brought to nought and there is bewilderment and helplessness in the face of irresistible calamity. Aeneas and the Trojan youth take up arms like ravening wolves driven by hunger and by the need to feed their famished young (lines 355–8). The simile suggests that the Trojan resistance is not so much heroic courage as desperation born of necessity and instinct. The image of the pack of wolves implies the predatory nature of their enterprise. When one of the Greek leaders, stumbling on these Trojans and mistaking them for Greeks, realises his error, he is like a man who steps on a snake and recoils in fright as it raises its head against him (lines 379–81). The sudden horror and fright affect Greeks as well as Trojans. The Greeks are an overwhelming force like winds clashing in a hurricane (lines 416–19). The image of the hurricane carries with it associations of violence, danger and confusion. Pyrrhus, before the threshold of Priam's palace, exults in his gleaming armour like a snake that, fed on poisonous herbs, emerges from its winter underground lair proudly exulting in its new skin and shooting its forky tongue (lines 471–5). Snakes are not always sinister in Virgil; in fact in Book 5 when the spirit of Anchises manifests itself in the form of a snake it is clearly a good omen, but here, although there is a fascination for the beauty of the beast shining exultantly in its new skin, the associations are predominantly sinister with the mention of the dark underground and the poisonous herbs. We are bound to associate the snake here with the monstrous serpents that killed Laocoon and with the lurking danger and horror of the snake that is stepped on at lines 379–81. The Greeks bursting into the palace are likened to a river bursting its banks and overwhelming all before it (lines 496–9). Hecuba and her daughters seek shelter like doves before a storm (lines 515–16). Troy in its fall is likened to an ancient ash tree on a mountain top which finally yields to the blows of woodsmen emulously striving to cut it down (lines 627–31). The tree is humanised and groans as the wounds are inflicted. Much is suggested here: the antiquity and eminence of Troy, the helplessness of the city, the magnitude and finality of its destruction, and the pain of it all.

THE SIMILES continued

The similes are not only in themselves vivid images which diversify the narrative but they are also fully integrated into its structure and feeling which they help to create and intensify. Notable in the similes of Book 2 is the repetition of the snake, and the recurrent emphasis upon the remorseless power of natural forces, together with the helpless bewilderment of the human onlooker faced with overwhelming violence and destruction.

PART FOUR

EXTENDED COMMENTARIES

TEXT 1 (BOOK 2 LINES 506–58)

Perhaps you may also ask how Priam died. When he saw the capture and fall of his city, the doors of his palace torn down and his enemy in the innermost sanctuary of his home, although he could achieve nothing, the old man buckled his armour long unused on shoulders trembling with age, girt on his feeble sword and made for the thick of the fight, looking for his death. In the middle of the palace, under the naked vault of heaven, there stood a great altar, and nearby an ancient laurel tree leaning over it and enfolding the household gods in its shade. Here, vainly embracing the images of the gods, Hecuba and her daughters were sitting flocked round the altar, like doves driven down in a black storm. When Hecuba saw that Priam had now put on his youthful armour, 'O my poor husband,' she cried, 'this is madness. Why have you put on this armour? Where can you go? This is not the sort of help we need. You are not the defender we are looking for. Not even my Hector, if he were here now … Just come here and sit by me. This altar will protect us all, or you will die with us.' As she spoke she took the old man to her and led him to a place by the holy altar.

Suddenly Polites, one of Priam's sons, came in sight. He had escaped death at the hands of Pyrrhus and now, wounded and with enemy weapons on every side, he was running through the long porticos of the palace and across the empty halls with Pyrrhus behind him in full cry, almost within reach, pressing him hard with his spear and poised to strike. As soon as he reached his father and mother, he fell and vomited his life's blood before their eyes. There was no escape for Priam. Death was now upon him, but he did not check himself or spare the anger in his voice. 'As for you,' he cried, 'and for what you have done, if there is any power in heaven that cares for such things, may the gods pay you well. May they give you the reward you have deserved for making me see my own son dying before my eyes, for defiling a father's face with the murder of his son. You pretend that Achilles was your father, but this is not how Achilles treated his enemy Priam. He had respect for my rights as a suppliant and for the trust I placed in him. He gave me back the bloodless body of Hector for burial and allowed me to return to the city where I was king.' With these words the old man feebly threw his harmless spear. It rattled on the bronze of Pyrrhus' shield and hung there useless sticking on the surface of the central boss. Pyrrhus then made his reply. 'In that case you will be my messenger and go to my father, son of Peleus. Let him know about my wicked deeds and do not forget to tell him about the degeneracy of his son Neoptolemus. Now, die.' As he spoke the word, he was dragging Priam to the very altar, his body trembling as it slithered through pools of his son's blood. Winding Priam's hair in his left hand, in his right he raised his sword with a flash of light and buried it to the hilt in Priam's side.

So ended the destiny of Priam. This was the death that fell to his lot. He who had once been the proud ruler over so many lands and peoples of Asia died with Troy ablaze before his eyes and the citadel of Pergamum in ruins. His mighty trunk lay upon the shore, the head hacked from the shoulders, a corpse without a name.

In telling the story of Troy's fall to Dido, Aeneas has reached the point at which the Greeks through the successful device of the Wooden Horse have penetrated the city at night and have reached the royal palace. Throughout the narrative, Aeneas has emphasised the remorseless power of fate, the futility of resistance and the inhumanity of the Greeks. Narrated from the Trojan point of view, the sack of the city is represented not as an heroic feat of arms but as the barbarous destruction of a great imperial city which brings out the worst in humanity.

The death of the Trojan king Priam, who is strongly identified in his age and enfeeblement with the city itself, is the climax of Aeneas's narrative of the pitiless and brutal fate of Troy and the Trojans. The merciless brutality is emphasised in the shaping of the narrative throughout. The actions and words of Priam and Hecuba are invested with great **pathos**. Priam, enfeebled by age, nevertheless attempts to put armour on his shaking shoulders, despite the obvious futility of the gesture which is pointed out to him by his wife. His age and venerability are reflected too in the description of the tree which gives shade to the altar at which Hecuba and the Trojan women have taken sanctuary. The **simile** in which they are likened to doves who have been driven down by a storm enhances their role as the innocent victims of a dark elemental force. Hecuba's words to Priam emphasise the futility of his feeble resistance and suggest that their only protection is to put their faith in the gods. However, the gods have deserted Troy, and the invading Greeks have no religious scruples. The description of the altar (and the repetition of the word which occurs four times in this opening paragraph) is not gratuitous, for Priam is subsequently killed over the altar with obvious **symbolic** effect: he becomes a sacrificial victim and the Greeks in Trojan eyes are guilty of horrendous sacrilege.

The brutality and pathos surrounding Priam's death are further intensified by the appalling spectacle presented when he and Hecuba are forced to witness the death of their son Polites at the hands of Pyrrhus, Achilles's son (also known as Neoptolemus). The brief description of the long chase provides an energetic contrast to the feebleness of Priam. Priam's words to Pyrrhus recall the encounter of the Trojan king with Achilles when he had visited the Greek camp to beg ransom for the body of his son Hector who had previously been killed by Achilles, which is the subject of the final book of Homer's *Iliad*. The allusion to the Homeric story is complex, for while Priam makes a just contrast with his former treatment by Achilles, it recalls the larger context of the *Iliad* in which Achilles had not only killed Hector (by fair means in one-to-one combat) but had then proceeded to abuse his corpse in murderous anger against the laws of gods and men, until the offended gods decide to put a stop to his sacrilege, by getting Hermes to conduct Priam to the Greek camp in disguise. Pyrrhus is therefore proving to be a true son of his father. The heavily sarcastic reply of the ruthless Pyrrhus actually seems to glory in the deed, and his dragging Priam to the altar makes the sacrilege purposeful. The physical circumstances of the old man's death, slithering through pools of his son's blood, are utterly repulsive. There is no glory in his death for victim or victor.

There is a moral point at the end. In Homer's *Iliad*, Achilles comes to see Priam and his own father Peleus as examples of the instability of human fortune. Virgil forces the point home with the narrative of Priam's ignominious death. The ignominy is intensified by the final description of his body as being decapitated and lying on the shore. This has been something of a crux, for Pyrrhus kills him over the altar and there has been no previous mention of decapitation. Commentators have suggested that Priam's body was subsequently removed from the city by the Greeks and further desecrated. There has also been the suggestion that Virgil is alluding to the death of Pompey the Great who, after he had been defeated in the civil war with Julius Caesar at the battle of Pharsalus in Greece (in 49BC), fled to Egypt where he was murdered and decapitated as he landed. The Egyptians doubtless wished to avoid the wrath of Caesar bearing down upon them. This allusion to recent history would further intensify the tragic fall from greatness already magnified by the poetic licence which leaves us with the image of the body of Priam as a nameless trunk on the shore.

TEXT 2   (BOOK 6 LINES 847–98)

'Others, I do not doubt it, will beat bronze into figures that breathe more softly. Others will draw living likenesses out of marble. Others will plead cases better or describe with their rod the courses of the stars across the sky and predict their risings. Your task, Roman, and do not forget it, will be to govern the peoples of the world in your empire. These will be your arts – and to impose a settled pattern upon peace, to pardon the defeated and war down the proud.'

Aeneas and the Sibyl wondered at what they heard, and Father Anchises continued: 'Look there at Marcellus marching in glory in spoils torn from the enemy commander he will fight and defeat. There he is, victorious and towering above all others. This is the man who will ride into battle and quell a great uprising, steadying the ranks of Rome and laying low the Carthaginian and the rebellious Gaul. He will be the third to dedicate the supreme spoils to Father Quirinus.'

At this Aeneas addressed his father, for he saw marching with Marcellus a young man, noble in appearance and in gleaming armour, but his brow was dark and his eyes downcast. 'Who is that, father, marching at the side of Marcellus? Is it one of his sons or one of the great line of his descendants? What a stir his escort makes! And himself, what a presence! But round his head there hovers a shadow dark as night.'

Then his father Anchises began to speak through his tears: 'O my son, do not ask. This is the greatest grief that you and yours will ever suffer. Fate will just show him to the earth – no more. The gods in heaven have judged that the Roman race would become too powerful if this gift were theirs to keep. What a noise of the mourning of men will come from the Field of Mars to Mars' great city. What a cortège will Tiber see as he glides past the new Mausoleum on his shore! No son of Troy will ever so raise the hopes of his Latin ancestors, nor will the land of

Romulus so pride itself on any of its young. Alas for his goodness! Alas for his old-fashioned truthfulness and that right hand undefeated in war! No enemies could ever have come against him in war and lived, whether he was armed to fight on foot or spurring the flanks of his foaming war-horse. Oh the pity of it! If only you could break the harsh laws of Fate! You will be Marcellus. Give lilies from full hands. Leave me to scatter red roses. These at least I can heap up for the spirit of my descendant and perform the rite although it will achieve nothing.'

So did they wander all over the broad fields of air and saw all there was to see, and after Anchises had shown each and every sight to his son and kindled in his mind a love for the glory that was to come, he told them of the wars he would have in due course to fight and of the Laurentine peoples, of the city of Latinus and how he could avoid or endure all the trials that lay before him.

There are two gates of sleep: one is called the Gate of Horn and it is an easy exit for true shades; the other is made all in gleaming white ivory, but through it the powers of the underworld send false dreams up towards the heavens. There on that night did Anchises walk with his son and with the Sibyl and spoke such words to them as he sent them on their journey through the Gate of Ivory.

Aeneas in the company of the Sibyl has descended into the underworld to meet the spirit of his recently deceased father Anchises. In a long speech, Anchises has shown Aeneas the roll call of his illustrious Roman descendants. The purpose of the speech in the overall design of the poem, made clear at the end, is to kindle in Aeneas's mind a love of the glory that is to come. At the climax he now articulates the destiny and mission of Rome. The others to whom he refers, though not directly named, are clearly understood to be the Greeks who excel in sculpture, oratory and science. Roman arts, by contrast, have to do with government and ruling. Here is the defining statement of the characteristic achievements of Greek and Roman civilisations. The triumphant tone disguises somewhat the clear admission of Roman cultural inferiority to the Greeks. Within this recognition is implied, though not directly stated, the inferiority of Roman literary achievements to those of the Greeks. The climax of the speech stresses not only Roman power but the ends served by Roman power, the justification for which is the *pax Romana*. For the arts of government and rule are not to be exercised for their own sake but as a means of imposing the habit of peace upon the world, a peace which, as it is merciful to the conquered and punishes the proud, entails a moral dimension.

Anchises then points to Marcellus, an early hero of Rome who had a distinguished military career against the Carthaginians and put down a rebellion in southern Gaul for which he won the *spolia opima*, the supreme spoils, awarded for only the third time in Roman history. This continues the theme of ancient heroism and distinguished service to the state that had previously featured in the roll call. But he is mentioned at this point chiefly to prepare us for what follows when Aeneas notices a noble youth marching beside him, his brows clouded in shades of night. Anchises does not immediately reveal his name but goes into a lament for Rome's misfortune in losing the promise of this youth in an early death. Virgil's first readers would immediately have recognised the youthful figure as alluding to Marcellus, the son of Augustus's sister and his designated successor, whose father was a descendant of the early hero, who had died in 23BC at the age of twenty. He was buried in a Mausoleum built by Augustus on the Campus Martius by the Tiber. He had already seen military service, hence the association of him with the military heroes of old Rome, the image of him fighting on foot or astride a foaming war-horse and the mention of Mars, god of war and father of the twins Romulus and Remus, one of the tutelary gods of Rome associated with the Martial character of Roman history and the Roman state. But the lament also associates him with other virtues, *pietas*, the central value of the poem here translated as 'goodness', and *prisca fides*, 'old-fashioned truthfulness'. Romans of Virgil's time looked back nostalgically to a time before they had been corrupted by the sophisticated luxuries that came with the acquisition of their great empire to the stern simplicity of their heroes of old. This return to old values is what is implied in the lament for Marcellus. The lament for him is particularly poignant because his death, seen through the perspective of prophecy, is fated and gives expression to one of the overriding themes of the whole poem, the inexorable and stern demands of fate felt equally by the Trojans, by the future Romans and by their enemies. The lament serves to mitigate the Roman triumphalism of Anchises's speech which ends as a consequence upon a more universal note. It also provides a fitting ending to the visit to the world of the dead in which Aeneas has heard about and witnessed so much suffering.

The lament provides the emotional climax of the journey to the underworld; the difficulties and dangers that lie ahead and are to be fully unfolded in the second half of the poem are only briefly alluded to, as trials that Aeneas can only avoid or endure. It is perhaps significant that Virgil does not show Aeneas responding with enthusiasm or indeed responding at all to the destiny laid out before him. His part in it is silently to acquiesce, avoiding what he can and enduring what he cannot avoid.

But it is not quite the end to this remarkable underworld journey, for the Sibyl leads Aeneas up to the light by way of the Ivory Gate, the gate of false dreams. This is one of the most remarkable moments of the whole poem. Despite some ingenious attempts, commentators have not been able to find a convincing explanation for what seems on the surface to be a very clear indication that the underworld dream, culminating in the desire to recreate the heroic past in the figure of Marcellus (even though that desire is not fulfilled) might well be an illusion.

TEXT 3   (BOOK 12 LINES 897–952)

He said no more but looked round and saw a huge rock, a huge and ancient rock which happened to be lying on the plain, a boundary stone put there to settle a dispute about land. Twelve picked men like those the earth now produces could scarcely lift it up on to their shoulders, but he caught it up in his trembling hands and, rising to his full height and running at speed, he hurled it at his enemy. But he had no sense of running or going, of lifting or moving the huge rock. His knees gave way. His blood chilled and froze and the stone rolled away under its own impetus over the open ground between them, but it did not go the whole way and it did not strike its target. Just as when we are asleep, when in the weariness of night, rest lies heavy on our eyes, we dream we are trying desperately to run further and not succeeding, till we fall exhausted in the middle of our efforts; the tongue is useless; the strength we know we have, fails our body; we have no voice, no words to obey our will – so it was with Turnus. Wherever his courage sought a way, the dread goddess barred his progress. During these moments, the thoughts whirled in his brain. He gazed at the Rutulians and the city. He faltered with fear. He began to tremble at the death that was upon him. He could see nowhere to run, no way to come at his enemy, no chariot anywhere, no sister to drive it.

As he faltered the deadly spear of Aeneas flashed. His eyes had picked the spot and he threw from long range with all his weight behind the throw. Stones hurled by siege artillery never roar like this. The crash of the burning thunderbolt is not so loud. Like a dark whirlwind it flew carrying death and destruction with it. Piercing the outer rings of the sevenfold shield and laying open the lower rim of the breastplate, it went whistling through the middle of the thigh. When the blow struck, down went great Turnus, bending his knee to the ground. The Rutulians rose with a groan which echoed round the whole mountain, and far and wide the high forests sent back the sound of their voices. He lowered his eyes and stretched out his right hand to beg as a suppliant. 'I have brought this upon myself,' he said, 'and for myself I ask nothing. Make use of what Fortune has given you, but if any thought of my unhappy father can touch you, I beg of you – and you too had such a father Anchises – take pity on the old age of Daunus, and give me back to my people, or if you prefer it, give them back my dead body. You have defeated me, and the men of Ausonia have seen me defeated and stretching out my hands to you. Lavinia is yours. Do not carry your hatred any further.'

There stood Aeneas, deadly in his armour, rolling his eyes, but he checked his hand, hesitating more and more as the words of Turnus began to move him, when suddenly his eyes caught the fatal baldric of the boy Pallas high on Turnus' shoulder with the glittering studs he knew so well. Turnus had defeated and wounded him and then killed him, and now he was wearing his belt on his shoulder as a battle honour taken from an enemy. Aeneas feasted his eyes on the sight of this spoil, this reminder of his own wild grief, then, burning with mad passion and terrible in his wrath, he cried: 'Are you to escape me now, wearing the spoils stripped from the body of those I loved? By this wound which I now give, it is Pallas who makes sacrifice of you. It is Pallas who exacts the penalty in your guilty blood.' Blazing with rage, he plunged the steel full into his enemy's breast. The limbs of Turnus were dissolved in cold and his life left him with a groan, fleeing in anger down to the shades.

The **epic** concludes with a one-to-one combat between the rival claimants for the hand of Lavinia, the leader of the incoming Trojans and the leader of the Italian resistance. The motif of the stone which can scarcely be lifted by twelve men of the present is a traditional epic device designed to raise the heroes of old in the audience's imagination. It is an **hyperbole** that contributes to the aggrandising style of epic. There is another later when the groan of the Rutulians echoes round the whole mountain while the high forests send back the sound far and wide. But Virgil has carefully adapted the traditional motif to the particular occasion of his narrative here. That Turnus should pick up a boundary stone that has been put there to settle a dispute about land is highly appropriate, given that this combat will also settle not merely the identity of Lavinia's bridegroom but also a larger dispute about land. The stone is also used to great effect to illustrate something about Turnus. Whereas traditionally the hero might prove his superior prowess by wielding such a stone, here the motif has the opposite effect: since Turnus cannot carry through his intention, it shows that he is not master of himself and marks a failure of self-knowledge – 'he had no sense of running or going'. The physical failure is also a psychological failure, reflected and intensified by the **simile** in which Turnus's plight is likened to the kind of paralysis we might experience in a nightmare. The simile internalises his crisis and creates great sympathy for the hero because it involves the reader with the use throughout of the personal pronoun 'we', and in its content represents a dilemma that can be felt by anyone and not merely by heroes. Finally, the use of the 'dread goddess' the *Dira* or Fury to block what his courage prompts is a reminder that fate is against him and cannot be eluded. He is on his own, with no sister (the nymph Juturna) to rescue him. At the critical moment, Virgil raises pity for him as a figure who is abandoned and completely trapped in an impasse from which there is no escape.

In the response of Aeneas, by contrast, performance fulfils intention: he is swift, purposeful and effective. The three short similes featuring the siege artillery, the burning thunderbolt and the dark whirlwind all magnify the physical effect. The speed of the narrative reflects the speed of the action. Turnus is quickly felled. When Achilles strikes Hector in the final combat of the *Iliad* on which this encounter is modelled, Hector receives a mortal blow, though he lives long enough to have final words with his foe. Here Turnus is wounded but the blow is not mortal. The wound forces him to kneel and he becomes a suppliant, admitting that he was wrong, yielding up his claim to Lavinia and begging for his life in the name of Anchises. The appeal almost works until Aeneas catches sight of the belt of Pallas, the young son of Evander who had committed him to Aeneas's care, whereupon he kills him in a fit of rage.

This moment has been long prepared for; when Turnus kills Pallas, exults over his body and seizes his belt as a spoil of war, Virgil intervenes in his narrative with the following sententious prophecy: 'The mind of man has no knowledge of what Fate holds in store, and observes no limit when Fortune raises him up. The time will come when Turnus would gladly pay, and pay richly, to see Pallas alive and unharmed. He will bitterly regret this spoil and the day he took it.' (Book 10, lines 501–5) Turnus's death makes a moral point.

But this is not all. The appeal that Turnus makes to Aeneas – that he should think of Anchises and have pity on the old age of his own father Daunus – recalls the comparable appeal made by Priam to Achilles, who reminds him of his own father Peleus (thus causing him to relent and release Hector's body), and also the earlier words of Anchises himself on the mission of Rome to quell the proud and spare the conquered. Turnus has been proud but is now humbled and as an unarmed suppliant he admits defeat, but he is not spared. Exacting revenge for the death of Pallas, Aeneas kills him 'burning with mad passion and terrible in his wrath'. In the last line of the poem the soul of Turnus departs 'fleeing in anger down to the shades'. The poem ends on a disquieting note of unappeased anger; in this respect it differs markedly from the *Iliad* at the end of which the anger is finally resolved.

The sympathy evoked for Turnus at the end, the clear image of him as a suppliant on bended knee with right had outstretched and the indignant departure of his unappeased spirit in the final line, together with the bitter anger shown by Aeneas (for he is not seen to feel the sweetness of revenge) that overrides the claims of mercy enjoined by Anchises – all these factors make the ending highly ambiguous in its emotional and moral effect. This ambiguity is not the result of confusion but the result of a highly sensitive intelligence refusing to close with easy answers to the complex problems of historical and human relations dramatised in his poem.

PART FIVE

Background

Virgil's life & works

Publius Vergilius Maro, traditionally called Virgil in English (though his name is sometimes spelt Vergil, following the form in which it appears in early manuscripts), was born in 70BC at the village of Andes near Mantua in that part of Italy north of the Po called in Roman times Transpadane. Like the majority of Latin writers, Virgil was therefore not Roman, and at the time of his birth the Transpadani unlike the rest of the Italians did not have full Roman citizenship. This they were granted in 49BC by Julius Caesar. Virgil's support for the Caesars may have had its roots in the local politics of his early years. Virgil's family was of humble origin, but his father owned land and had sufficient means to see that Virgil was well educated, first at Cremona, then at Milan and finally at Rome. He learned Greek and studied philosophy and **rhetoric** under the most notable teachers of the day. He made one appearance as an advocate in the courts but then retired to Naples where he studied philosophy and began his literary career. He made his name with the publication in 37BC of the *Eclogues,* ten **pastoral** poems loosely modelled upon the Greek poems of the Sicilian Theocritus. According to tradition, the first eclogue records Virgil's gratitude to Octavian (later Augustus) for restoring his father's farm which had been appropriated in 41BC for war veterans. The so-called 'Messianic' eclogue (the fourth) celebrates the birth of a child who will restore the Golden Age to Italy. Thereafter Virgil was a member of literary circle of Maecenas, the great patron of the arts and associate of Octavian. Virgil continued to enjoy this patronage for the rest of his life, and was able to live as a man of letters without the need to earn a living by any other means. In 29BC he finished the *Georgics,* a poem in four books, **genre** treating various aspects of country life and farming. In Book 3 he acknowledges his debt to Maecenas (line 41) and declares that he will one day sing Caesar's praises (lines 46–8). The **epic** poem, the *Aeneid,* his last work, was composed over a number of years. It was unfinished when he died in 19BC. According to his ancient biographer Donatus he began from a prose outline divided into twelve books which he then filled out as his inclination prompted him and not according to the order of design. The occasional presence throughout the poem of half lines makes this account seem likely. The uncompleted lines indicate that Virgil had not yet quite integrated the parts into a seamless whole. It is not generally believed, however, that its overall design was in any significant way unfinished, or that he would have added more to the narrative or changed the ending, if he had lived longer. His method of composition, according to the ancient account, may be relevant here. He is said to have composed a number of lines in the morning and revised them in the course of the day, reducing their number in the process. This is the method of the laboriously perfectionist artist (he spent ten years on the *Georgics*). What the poem may be said to lack is the final artistic touch of the perfectionist, his *ultima manus*, his final hand of revision. This is the sense in which it is unfinished. He had given orders to his executors that it should be burnt if he died before completing it. However, Augustus, to whom Virgil had read Books 2, 4 and 6, ordered that the poem be published in its unfinished form.

THE POLITICAL BACKGROUND & THE AUGUSTAN AGE

In Virgil's lifetime the Roman state underwent a major revolutionary change. The Roman Republic, which had replaced the monarchy and lasted for 400 years, was replaced in its turn by the imperial government of Rome's first emperor, Augustus Caesar (68BC–AD14). In the old Republican constitution, supreme executive power was invested in the consuls, two magistrates nominated by the Senate and elected by the people, who held office on an equal basis for one year only. They were customarily members of the landed aristocracy from whose ranks the 300 senators were also largely drawn. The acquisition of a large empire brought with it the need for institutional change which the ruling senatorial aristocracy failed to make. Consequently the 100 years prior to Augustus were characterised by internal disorder and the abuse of military power, resulting in frequent civil wars and violent subversion of the constitution. Just before Virgil's birth there had been a major civil war between competing generals which resulted in the dictatorship of Cornelius Sulla (138–78BC) with his infamous proscription lists of his personal enemies who might be killed with impunity.

Virgil's early life saw the rise to prominence of Julius Caesar (100–44BC), the conspiracy of Catiline in 63BC (see *Aeneid*, Book 8, line 668) and the establishment of the first triumvirate in 60BC, an unconstitutional arrangement whereby the three most powerful men of the time, Julius Caesar, Pompey (106–48BC) and Crassus (d.53BC), divided the government of the Roman world among them. After the death of Crassus in 53BC, relations between the two remaining triumvirs deteriorated until Julius Caesar declared war on Pompey and the Senate by crossing the Rubicon with his legions and invading Italy from Gaul in 49BC (see *Aeneid*, Book 6, lines 826–35). After the elimination of Pompey, Julius Caesar became dictator for life and the ruler of the Roman world. He was assassinated in a conspiracy in the name of the Republican government led by his former friends and supporters Brutus and Cassius in 44BC. After Caesar's death, his leading supporters, Mark Antony (83–31BC), Lepidus (d.12BC) and Octavian (68BC–AD14), Caesar's great nephew and heir, formed the second triumvirate, whereby the government of the Roman world was to be divided between them. Proscriptions followed in which many of their political opponents perished, including Mark Antony's great antagonist, the famous Roman orator Cicero (106–43BC). Other Republicans led by Brutus and Cassius were defeated at the battle of Philippi in 42BC. Antony then undertook the task of restoring order in the East while Octavian controlled Italy and the western provinces. Lepidus, the least powerful of the three, was given Africa, until deprived of his command by Octavian in 35BC.

Antony spent his time in the East either in abortive campaigns against the Parthians who were a threat to Rome's eastern provinces, or at the Egyptian court, where, like Julius Caesar before him he was regally entertained by the Egyptian queen Cleopatra who in effect became his mistress (see *Aeneid*, Book 8, line 688). When Antony dissolved his marriage to Octavia with which he had earlier cemented his alliance with her brother Octavian, rivalry between the two triumvirs reached breaking point. Octavian denounced Antony in the Senate, and in 32BC war was declared, ostensibly upon Cleopatra. In a naval engagement at Actium in 31BC Cleopatra's forces deserted in the midst of the fighting; Antony followed her, so losing the battle, his fleet and most of his followers

(*Aeneid*, Book 8, lines 691–713). Octavian moved against Egypt where Antony, hearing a false report of Cleopatra's death, committed suicide. To avoid the indignity of being exhibited in a Roman triumph, Cleopatra followed his example, and Egypt became a Roman province. Octavian returned to Rome and celebrated a triple triumph for victories in Dalmatia, at Actium and in Egypt. As a victorious general, he was allowed to bring his army into the city and ride up to the Capitol as the representative of Jupiter Capitolinus (*Aeneid*, Book 8, lines 714–28). The temple of Janus, open in time of war and closed in time of peace, was formally closed in 29BC for only the third time in Roman history, a **symbolic** act which was to inaugurate a new age of peace (*Aeneid*, Book 1, line 294).

After the battle of Actium, Octavian, like Julius Caesar before him, was the sole master of the Roman world. In 27BC he formally renounced the unconstitutional powers he had held as triumvir. He took the additional name of Augustus, becoming Caius Julius Caesar Octavianus Augustus. He had all the powers held by Julius Caesar – in particular the armed forces all swore allegiance to him as Imperator, Commander-in-chief – but, aiming by all means to reconcile the Romans to his rule, he disguised his powers under traditional Republican forms. Indeed he claimed to have restored the Republic. The old Republican liberty, however, was a thing of the past. He was hailed as first citizen, Princeps, from which his rule is often referred to as the principate. He later became Pontifex Maximus, chief priest, and so was the religious as well as the civil and military head of state. When Julius Caesar had been declared a god in 42BC, Octavian, who had taken Julius Caesar's name on being adopted as his heir, became '*filius divi*', 'son of a god', and is so described on coins (see *Aeneid*, Book 6, line 792). After his death, he was deified by decree of the Senate, and in his lifetime he discreetly encouraged worship of his Genius (the companion spirit that accompanied every Roman through life), particularly in the Eastern provinces. In Rome, however, he lived simply and modestly without undue pomp and ceremony. Augustus had no son and in 23BC his son-in-law Marcellus died (*Aeneid*, Book 6, lines 867–86). He was eventually succeeded in AD14 by his stepson Tiberius whom he had made his heir, as he himself had been made Julius Caesar's heir. A semblance of Republican tradition was kept up in that the principate was never strictly hereditary, and the new emperor was nominally invested with his powers by the Senate and people in the way in which the magistracies had traditionally been elected and confirmed.

In the course of eliminating his rival Antony, Augustus had brought Dalmatia (now Yugoslavia) under Roman control and made Egypt into a Roman province, but after he had gained supreme power, the main object of his foreign policy was to consolidate inherited gains and secure existing frontiers rather than acquire new territory. In the West, Julius Caesar had established Roman rule in Gaul from the Alps to the Rhine during his campaigns of 58–51BC, while Augustus himself directed the urbanisation of Gaul and Spain. Pompey had rid the eastern seas of pirates and defeated Mithridates of Pontus. Augustus consolidated Roman power in the East by making peace with Parthia after one of his generals had restored Roman pride by recovering the standards lost to the Parthians by Crassus in 53BC (see *Aeneid*, Book 7, line 606). Another of Augustus's generals defeated the Garamantes in Africa in 19BC (see *Aeneid*, Book 6, line 794) who then made a treaty with Rome securing the Egyptian frontier. Augustus also received friendly embassies from various nations recognising Roman authority, including India (see *Aeneid*, Book 6, line 794). After more than a century of discord, upheaval and near chaos at home and abroad, Augustus had, therefore, settled the Roman state and gradually brought peace, order and security to Rome and her dominions. In its essential elements, the Augustan imperial settlement with its revised constitution at home and its imposed peace abroad (*Aeneid*, Book 6, lines 851–3) endured for four centuries.

In domestic affairs, Augustus, a true Roman in his conservative political instincts, made changes that had a strongly traditional appeal. As he had 'restored' the Republic, so he set about restoring the ancient religion, rebuilding eighty-two temples in and around the city of Rome. He associated himself with ancient religious orders such as the Salii (*Aeneid*, Book 8, line 285) and the Luperci (*Aeneid*, Book 8, line 633) and he also founded three new temples. The first, symbolising the source of his power and authority, was to Mars Ultor, the avenging deity of the murdered Julius Caesar. The second was to Apollo in 28BC (see *Aeneid*, Book 6, lines 69–70) with whom Augustus associated his victory at Actium (*Aeneid*, Book 8, line 704). The third was to Vesta, goddess of the hearth and symbol of the undying life of the city (see *Aeneid*, Book 2, line 296), so that the spirit of Rome was henceforward closely associated with the imperial family. The building of these temples was part of a general restoration whereby Augustus had 'found Rome brick, left it marble'. In moral legislation to encourage family life and to curb excessive private wealth, Augustus also appealed to traditional Roman ways (the *mores maiorum*), invoking the ancestral spirit in all he set out to do.

Augustus had devoted his enormous personal wealth to public works, and his munificence raised magnificent monuments to Roman imperial grandeur. The literary arts were fostered through the patronage of his friend Maecenas. Oratory, history and drama suffered with the loss of freedom, but, under imperial patronage, poetry flourished. The foremost Augustans, Virgil and his fellow poet Horace (65–8BC), heralded the transformation of the Roman state under Augustus, identified themselves with the new order and gave expression to the mood of self-confidence generated by the Augustan peace. Their art was thoroughly Roman in character, but like the Roman achievement it assimilated much from the past. In particular both these poets endeavoured to bring to bear upon Roman culture the artistic ideals of the Hellenestic age (the period from the death of Alexander the Great in 323BC to the Roman conquest of Greece in the second century) with an emphasis upon breadth of learning and the cultivation of an artistic refinement and polish. However, there was no question of art for art's sake: Augustan art was to express the ideals and the deepest moral concerns of the Augustan age.

THE CULTURAL BACKGROUND & VIRGIL'S ROMAN PREDECESSORS

Literature and the arts developed late at Rome. The Roman state existed for five centuries without producing any serious literature worthy of the name. In these early days the Romans were an agricultural community, land-based in their occupations and their military organisation. The legion was their great strength; they did not develop a navy or the commercial interests to take them overseas and extend their horizons. The art of public speaking was prized in their Republican constitution, and their highly developed legal system was the product of intellectual skills of a practical kind, but speculative thinking or imaginative literature did not come naturally to the Romans. Their neglect of art is apparent in their language in which there is no native Latin word for poet. The primary meaning of the word *vates*, which later came to be used for 'poet', is prophet or seer; similarly *carmen*, later 'song', is initially a prophetic utterance. The word *poeta* the Romans imported like their art and their philosophy from the Greeks. The Romans remained borrowers, so that in philosophy and science they produced no great original minds, and in architecture, sculpture, painting and literature they laboriously adapted Greek originals to Roman purposes.

The first serious attempts at a national literature were made when the Romans came into direct contact with Greek culture. There had been indirect influence from early times, since Rome in its early centuries was simply a small power in a world dominated by Greek culture which had spread widely in the Mediterranean. There had been early Greek colonies in Sicily, on the coast of southern Italy in what was called Magna Graecia, and as far north as Campania. The richest of such colonies and settlements transmitted knowledge of Classical Greek literature, philosophy and science from the fifth and fourth centuries, and their architecture, sculpture, painting and pottery were frequently in the best traditions of Greek art. However, there were no Greek settlements in Latium, and the Romans were at first isolated by other Italians, notably the Sabines, from direct contact with such settlements, but as they became the dominant power in Italy in the third century, so they came into direct contact with Italian Greeks.

Roman ascendancy in Italy dates from the capture in 271BC of Tarentum, a rich Greek city on the coast of Calabria in the south. One of those captured was a Greek named Andronicus who was taken to Rome as the slave of the noble family Livii. As a reward for teaching his master's sons, Andronicus was given his freedom, and he took the name of his patron. He stayed at Rome and as a freedman continued to teach, mastering Latin himself in the process. Greek children started their schooling by reading the **epic** poet Homer. As there was no Roman equivalent, Andronicus translated Homer's *Odyssey* into Latin. Homer, who had educated the Greeks, now began to educate the Romans. Two hundred years later the Latin *Odyssey* of Livius Andronicus was still being used as a schoolbook as the testimony of Virgil's friend Horace shows (*Ars Poetica,* 69–71). Andronicus went on to translate Greek plays, and his translations were adapted for the Roman stage, being the first of their kind to be performed at Rome. The career of Livius Andronicus, a Greek slave who became half-Latin and went on to educate Roman children and become the first Latin author, is prophetic of the whole course of subsequent cultural relations between the Romans and the Greeks. In a literal sense, the Romans were educated by the Greeks. Their sons continued to be schooled for the most part by bilingual tutors of Greek origin. But in introducing the masterpieces of Greek epic and tragedy to Rome, Andronicus started the process by which in a deeper sense Greece educated Rome. As Horace expressed it, 'conquered Greece itself took its savage conqueror captive and brought the arts to uncultivated Latium' (Epistle 2, 156).

The first original Roman poem was written by Gnaeus Naevius, a native of Campania, where there were established Greek settlements and recent Roman colonies. He was a Roman soldier in the first Punic War between Rome and Carthage of 264–241 BC, a war between the two dominant powers in the Mediterranean which brought Rome for the first time into close contact with the rich Greek culture of Sicily. Like Andronicus he adapted Greek plays for the Roman stage, but his main claim to fame rests with his poem called the *Punic War*. Fragments survive from which it is clear that he mixed myth and history as Virgil was to do later. He used the myth of Aeneas to trace the origins of the Romans to Troy, described the Trojans' wanderings (as Virgil does in *Aeneid*, Book 3) and has the Trojans land at Carthage where they meet Dido (like Virgil in *Aeneid*, Book 1). He thereby laid the foundation of the national epic upon which Virgil was to build in the *Aeneid*.

Naevius had concentrated upon a single episode in Rome's past, but the next epic, the *Annals* of Ennius, attempted the entire history of Rome from its beginning. Quintus Ennius was born at Rudiae in Calabria in southern Italy and so was half Greek by origin. He fought in the second Punic War, in which Rome defeated the Carthaginians and emerged as the dominant Mediterranean power. Like Andronicus and Naevius, Ennius made his living at Rome by teaching and by translating and adapting Greek plays for the Roman stage. The poem of Ennius was remarkable for its scope, and for the fact that whereas Andronicus and Naevius had used the native Latin metre called the Saturnian, Ennius adopted the Greek epic metre used by Homer, the **hexameter**. The Greek and specifically Homeric inspiration is further apparent in the vision at the opening of the poem in which the spirit of Homer tells Ennius that he is Homer's reincarnation. From Homer, too, he derived a council of the Gods (compare *Aeneid*, Book 1, lines 223–96 and Book 10, lines 1–117). One of Horace's cardinal precepts in his *Art of Poetry* is the injunction to his contemporaries: 'read Greek models by night, read them by day' (line 268). Latin poets had been doing this from the beginning, as early Roman literature evolved from the translation, adaptation and imitation of Greek models. With Ennius the dominance of Greek forms is complete. The Saturnian metre was never again used for serious literature.

The growth of a national literature based upon absorption of the great masterpieces of Greece came naturally with the spread of Roman power. For the purposes of administration and convenience the Romans soon found that they needed a knowledge of Greek. With power there also came wealth, and with wealth an opportunity for leisure, a necessary prerequisite for the development of culture. Actual contact with the great centres of Greek civilisation in Sicily and mainland Greece stimulated an appetite for Greek culture among leading Romans such as the Scipios who developed a genuine enthusiasm for Greek philosophy, art and literature. Foreign conquest brought with it an extension of Roman consciousness beyond the bounds of their own rather narrow inheritance. That inheritance had served them well in the development of civil and military institutions. They acquired their dominion in the first place by virtue of the superior efficiency and discipline of the legion as a fighting force, a fighting force that remained effectively within the control of the civil power. But to maintain their dominion, more than discipline and efficiency was needed. The Romans succeeded in part because they were flexible enough to develop a policy whereby those who came under their power could also enjoy its benefits. Livius Andronicus was a Greek slave who gained his freedom, Ennius an Italian provincial who was granted Roman citizenship. But they succeeded also because they were prepared to expand their national horizons. The extension of privileges to non-Romans was matched by a capacity for assimilating what they had to offer. There was, however, some resistance to the assimilation of Greek culture. In 161BC Marcus Porcus Cato succeeded in procuring the banishment of all Greek philosophers and rhetoricians from Rome on the grounds that Greek influence was undermining the solidity of the old

Roman character. Nevertheless this was only a temporary halt to the gradual metamorphosis of the Roman into the Graeco-Roman.

The assimilation and absorption of Greek literature by the Romans are an extension, perhaps the fulfilment, of a long process of more gradual acceptance of Greek influence at Rome. The Romans had little native mythology and the deities of the old Roman religion were comparatively colourless and abstract. When they encountered the more colourful and imaginative creations of the Greeks, the Romans readily assimilated them, identifying their own deities with the Olympian gods of Greece: Saturn with Cronos, for example, or Jupiter with Zeus. In time both their ideas about the gods and their mode of worship were transformed according to the Greek model. They worshipped in temples in the style of the Greeks or of the Etruscans who had similarly adopted Greek ways, and the images of their gods were derived ultimately from Greek sculpture. They also imported new cults from Greece. Worship of Apollo, the god most closely associated with Greek culture, was introduced to Rome in 431BC (see *Aeneid*, Book 6, lines 69–70). Shortly after the defeat of Carthage, worship of the great mother Cybele was imported from Asia Minor in 201BC, the first of many such Oriental cults to come to Rome through Greece (see *Aeneid*, Book 6, line 784). Many of the legends which circulated among the Romans in later times were borrowed from or inspired by the Greeks, possibly through the mediating influence of the Etruscans.

The myth of Aeneas, used by Naevius in the first original Latin poem and accepted as canonical by other Latin writers before Virgil, was, of course, Greek in origin, even if it connects the Romans with the enemies of Greece, the Trojans. In fact the myth **symbolises** well the Graeco-Roman character of the developing culture of Rome. Aeneas first appears in Homer's *Iliad*, Book 20, line 305 where it is predicted that he and his children's children will one day rule the Trojans. The story of Aeneas's wanderings from Troy occurs in subsequent Greek writers and we may believe that Aeneas was first connected with Italy by the Greeks themselves, by Homer's successors who continued the saga of the Trojans where he had left off. One of these continuators, whose work collectively is often referred to as the Epic Cycle, the fifth-century Greek writer Hellanicus, does indeed make this connection. However, from fragments of surviving vases it is clear that the legend of Aeneas was known in

Etruria as early as the late sixth century BC. The inhabitants of Italy were thereby connected with the predominant Mediterranean civilisation, while at the same time allowed their own distinct and separate identity, since, through the myth of Aeneas, they were derived from an older civilisation eclipsed by the Greeks. Moreover, in the form in which it was accepted at Rome, the legend expresses the idea of assimilation rather than subjugation or conquest, since Aeneas marries into the existing Latin stock, so that his descendants are derived equally from Latins and Trojans. We may suppose that the development of the legend at Rome marked the broadening growth of foreign influence, which radically affected the Romans' ideas about themselves and their place in the world.

In adapting the Greek tradition, Virgil followed the example of his Roman predecessors in epic, Naevius and Ennius, but in the extent to which he makes use of it he goes far beyond them. Naevius used the myth of Aeneas and introduced Homer's gods into his *Punic War*. As Thetis petitioned Zeus for her son Achilles in the *Iliad* (Book 1, lines 495–527), Naevius makes Venus complain to Jupiter about the treatment of her son Aeneas in a storm raised by Juno (compare *Aeneid*, Book 1, lines 229–53). In the *Annals* of Ennius, Jupiter is closely associated with the Romans and Juno champions the cause of Carthage. Her hostility to Rome is only appeased after the second Punic War (compare *Aeneid*, Book 1, lines 279–82 and Book 10, lines 11–14). But although they start with myth, Naevius and Ennius are both primarily interested in writing an historical poem. Their narratives have a straightforward chronological sequence and are clearly designed to culminate in the events of their own time.

PART SIX

CRITICAL HISTORY & FURTHER READING

ANTIQUITY & THE MIDDLE AGES

Virgil's works almost immediately became school texts and, wherever Latin has been seriously studied since, they have occupied a primary place in the curriculum. There are celebrated ancient commentaries, often accompanying the text in manuscripts and early printed editions, by the grammarians Donatus and Servius from the fifth century. They form the basis of subsequent commentary in elucidating mythological references and explaining points of grammar and syntax, as well as offering interpretative comment on particular words, phrases and lines, and citing parallel passages from other Greek or Roman poets. There are also two lives of Virgil, both attributed to Donatus, which were written several centuries after the poet's death, but which may contain material that is genuinely historical. From the outset, Virgil's relationship to predecessors, particularly to Homer in the *Aeneid*, was the subject of investigation, the most notable being the extensive sixth-century comparison between the two poets written by Ambrosius Theodosius Macrobius in his *Saturnalia* (Book 5).

A famous early testimony is that of the Christian Archbishop Augustine of Hippo (354–430) who recorded in his *Confessions* (*c*.395) that he had wept over the fate of Dido (Book 1. 13). In his later *City of God*, written just after Rome had been sacked by Alaric the Goth (in 410) he questioned the prophecy of Jupiter that the Romans would enjoy *imperium sine fine* (*Aeneid*, Book 1, line 279) 'empire without end'. Although the Western empire finally fell in 476, Latin continued to be the language of learning and the church, so that the *Aeneid* continued to be read long after the fall of Rome into the Middle Ages. With the dissolution of the empire national interest in the Roman theme declined, but medieval readers identified strongly with Virgil's contempt of the world and saw in the journey and travail of Aeneas an **allegorical** representation of man's earthly pilgrimage through this vale of tears. Rome, which is always in the future for Aeneas, might be the **symbol** of the *summum bonum* ('the highest good') or of the heavenly city not to be attained in this world. One such medieval allegory on these lines to survive is attributed to Bernard Silvestris in the twelfth century. The awkward fact that Virgil as a pagan might not himself have attained the heavenly city is acknowledged by Dante (1265–1321) who makes Virgil his guide (rather as the Sibyl had been the guide of Aeneas through Hades) in his *Inferno* (*c*.1310) but does not allow him into paradise. Dante's Virgil is a good pagan and the supreme representative of the best in pagan culture, '*l'altissimo poeta*', ' the loftiest poet' (Canto IV, 80), and author of '*lo bello stile*', 'the beautiful style' (Canto 1, 87), but nevertheless has to stay in a special limbo reserved for those who had lived good lives but had not received the revelation directly. On the other hand, Virgil's so-called 'Messianic' eclogue (Pastoral 4), in which the poet prophesies the birth of a child who will bring peace to the world and restore the Golden Age, was often interpreted in the early Christian era as a prophecy of the birth of Christ, and so made Virgil into a kind of pagan John the Baptist and a mediator between pagan and Christian dispensations. At the same time allegorical interpretation of the *Aeneid* could suggest that Virgil's poetry anticipates Christian truths which can be discerned under the veil of pagan fictions. This allegorical approach, which in the case of other myths in other poets might produce strained and indeed bizarre interpretations, did not necessarily go counter to the spirit of the *Aeneid*, the main value of which, *pietas*, might easily sound like a religious or spiritual virtue. For the modern critic T.S. Eliot, Aeneas is 'the prototype of a Christian hero. For he is, humbly, a man with a mission; and the mission is everything'. Eliot continues: 'We find the world of Virgil, compared to the world of Homer, to approximate to a Christian world, in the choice, order and relationship of its values. ... Virgil is uniquely near to Christianity'. He then appropriates to Virgil a phrase drawn from one of the early Church fathers, Tertullian, *anima naturaliter Christiana*, 'a naturally Christian soul'.

FURTHER READING
C. Baswell, *Virgil in Medieval England: Figuring the Aeneid from the Twelfth Century to Chaucer*, Cambridge University Press, 1995
> A detailed scholarly account of medieval annotation of manuscripts of the *Aeneid*

Domenico Comparetti, *Vergil in the Middle Ages*, translated by E.F.M. Benecke, with a new introduction by Jan M. Ziolkowski, University of Princeton Press, 1997

> The standard work first written in 1885 now reissued: a mine of information

T.S. Eliot, 'Virgil and the Christian World'[1951], *On Poetry and Poets*, Faber, 1957

> Includes discussion of Virgil and Dante

J.K. Jones, 'The Allegorical Traditions of the *Aeneid*', in *Vergil at 2000: Commemorative Essays on the Poet and his Influence*, edited by John D. Bernard, AMS Press, New York, 1986

> Divided into two section: I The Classical Tradition II The Medieval Tradition

G.N. Knauer, 'Vergil's *Aeneid* and Homer', *Greek, Roman and Byzantine Studies*, 5, 1964, pp. 61–84

> Sums up a fuller study of Virgil's use of Homer in the tradition of Macrobius

Ambrosii Theodosii Macrobii Saturnalia, edited by Jacob Willis, Teubner, 1963; *Macrobius: The Saturnalia*, translated with an Introduction and notes by Percival Vaughan Davies, Records of Civilisation: Sources and Studies, New York, 1969

> A substantial comparison with comment from the Roman grammatical tradition

THE RENAISSANCE & EIGHTEENTH CENTURY

Many medieval habits continued in the **Renaissance**; the most thoroughgoing **allegorical** exposition of the poem, for example, is by the Renaissance Florentine humanist Cristofero Landino (*c*.1424–*c*.98) However, in the Renaissance there were also two new emphases.

The first interest results from the desire of these early humanists to reform Latin which continued to be the language of the church, the universities and the courts by purging it of what they regarded as the barbarisms that it had acquired through the ages, in an attempt to go back to the purer style of the Romans themselves. This classical revival led to the elevation of certain canonical classical texts as models and authorities for exemplary classical practice. Virgil had always been regarded as a supreme model for classical **hexameter** practice and a master of **rhetoric** and of the grand style, all exemplified to their most sublime effect in the *Aeneid*. His poetry has retained such a status wherever Latin has been studied to an advanced level in schools and universities to the present day. In the Renaissance the *Aeneid* was studied ever more systematically as a classical model for would-be poets aspiring to write in a dignified style, whether in neo-Latin or in the vernacular languages.

The second Renaissance interest centres upon a revival of interest in the national character and the Roman theme of the *Aeneid*, particularly amongst the Italians who saw themselves as the heirs of the old Romans. When the Italian **humanists** (that is, those who saw an intrinsic value in the Greek and Latin classics) rediscovered the lost grandeur of ancient Rome (in a quite literal way, they dug up and collected Roman remains), they shared all the enthusiasm for their Roman past that Anchises expresses for the Roman future in Book 6. One of their number, the Latin scholar Maphaeus Vegius (1407–58), seeing something incomplete in the *Aeneid*, added a thirteenth book, which was regularly reprinted in Renaissance editions of Virgil. In it Aeneas is rewarded for his pains, celebrates his marriage to Lavinia, and founds his city where he lives happily until he is received into the bosom of the gods. So Vegius imagined Virgil would have concluded his poem had he lived to complete it, even if it may now be thought that such an ending goes quite counter to the spirit of the *Aeneid*. Vegius's supplement also reflects an aspect of a new secular and historical interest in the poem on the part of Renaissance readers who became newly attuned to its **Augustan** political context and to what they considered its Augustan political purpose. The view that Aeneas foreshadowed Augustus became commonplace, as did, likewise, the political moral of the poem which is expressed with succinct clarity by John Dryden (1631–1700) in the introduction to his translation of 1697. Virgil, he argued, having 'maturely weighed the condition of his times' and reflecting that Augustus as conqueror 'though of a bad kind, was the very best of it' concluded that it was in the national interest 'to infuse an awful respect into the people towards such a prince; by that respect to confirm their obedience to him, and by that obedience to make them happy. This was the moral of his divine poem'. Despite this in the act of translating the poem Dryden, who produced the best version in English, was not insensitive to the poem's political complexities.

Examples from this version have been cited in the section on Language & Style in Critical Approaches.

FURTHER READING

D.C. Allen, *Mysteriously Meant. The Rediscovery of Pagan Symbolism and Allegorical Interpretation in the Renaissance*, John Hopkins University Press, 1970

> Contains a chapter on the *Aeneid*

Anna Cox Brinton, *Mapheus Vegius and his Thirteenth Book of the Aeneid*, Garland Publishing, 1978

> Includes the text, a translation and full notes and introduction

Robert Cummings, "'To the cart the fift quheill": Gavin Douglas's Humanist Supplement to the *Eneados'*, *Translation & Literature*, 4:2 pp. 131–156

> Discusses translation and politics in relation to both Vegius and Douglas

K.W. Gransden, 'The *Aeneid* and *Paradise Lost'*, in *Virgil and his Influence: Bimillennial Studies*, edited by Charles Martindale, Bristol Classical Press, 1984

> Includes a useful section on the influence of Virgil on Milton's style

Paul Hammond, *Dryden and the Traces of Classical Rome*, Oxford University Press, 1999

> Includes a chapter entitled 'The Epic of Exile' on Dryden's translation of the *Aeneid*

T.W. Harrison, 'English Virgil: the *Aeneid* in the XVIII century', *Philologica Pragensia* 10, 1967, pp. 1–11 and 80–91

> A study of translations

Robin Sowerby, *Dryden's Aeneid: A Selection with Introduction and Commentary*, Bristol Classical Press, 1986

> A substantial selection designed for students and beginners

THE ROMANTIC ERA & NINETEENTH CENTURY

In the **Renaissance** and in the **neoclassical** era (*c.*1660–*c.*1780), the Roman poets in general and Virgil in particular were the principal classical models and held in the highest esteem. With the advent of **Romanticism**, there was a perceptible shift in the relative valuation of Greek and Roman culture, with much more attention and emphasis given to the Greeks who came to be regarded as the great originators at the expense of their Roman counterparts who were often depreciated as pale imitators. Virgil was affected less than other Roman writers, but even so there were those who stressed the derivativeness of Virgil in favour of the original genius of Homer, particularly in relation to the **epic** where Virgil's debt to Homer is very obvious for all to see. Homer was also felt to be genuinely nearer to the essential folkways of the Greeks than Virgil was to Roman origins. For Romantics who valued the primitive, Virgil might seem over-literary and the *Aeneid* to be artificially concocted from secondary sources. (This was particularly true in Germany.) There was too a movement away from classical models and greater emphasis in Romantic poetry upon the self and upon private experience, and a feeling that the public poetry of the **Augustans** in epics and odes was less in tune with contemporary aspirations and modes than had previously been the case. It was in the Romantic era that the notion was first promulgated that Virgil, in undertaking an epic at the behest of his Augustan patron Maecenas, had betrayed his true genius which was essentially for lyric.

Although in the imperial times of the nineteenth century the imperial strain in the *Aeneid* often resonated strongly, for many of the most sensitive critics and readers at this time it was the melancholy side of the poem that struck a deeper chord than its grand design. Matthew Arnold's verdict in his essay 'On the Modern Element in Literature' is a case in point: 'Over the whole of the great poem of Virgil, over the *Aeneid*, there rests an ineffable melancholy; … a melancholy which is at once a source of charm in the poem, and a testimony to its incompleteness'. Much was made of the famous utterance of Aeneas when he gazes upon the scenes of Trojan suffering pictured on the walls of the temple of Juno at Carthage: *'Sunt hic etiam sua praemia laudi, / Sunt lacrimae rerum, et mentem mortalia tangunt'* (Book 1, lines 461–2) 'Here too there is just reward for merit, there are tears for suffering and men's hearts are touched by what man has to bear'. The translation here does not quite capture what readers saw in the phrase *lacrimae rerum* 'tears inherent in things'. Worth noting here are the emphases of Alfred

Tennyson (1809–92) in his fine poetic tribute 'To Virgil', written in 1882 for the nineteenth centenary of Virgil's death:

Thou that seest Universal
    Nature moved by Universal Mind;
Thou majestic in thy sadness
    at the doubtful doom of human kind;

Light among the vanish'd ages;
    star that gildest yet this phantom shore;
Golden branch amid the shadows,
    kings and realms that pass to rise no more;

Now thy Forum roars no longer,
    fallen every purple Caesar's dome –
Tho' thine ocean-roll of rhythm
    sound for ever of imperial Rome –

The Universal Mind must be prompted by Anchises's speech beginning *'spiritus intus alit, totamque infusa per artus/mens agitat molem'* (Book 6, lines 726–7): 'Spirit fed all things from within … It was Mind that set all this matter in motion'. This is a prelude to the roll-call of Aeneas's illustrious descendants, still phantom spirits, who will eventually impose the *pax Romana* upon the waiting world. In Tennyson the great imperial theme, with the loss of the Roman empire, is invoked indirectly as it is transformed into the imperial splendour of Virgil's stately and magisterial 'ocean roll of rhythm'. The spirits themselves have also become **metaphorical** while the golden bough becomes a figure for the poet himself who can give us privileged access to the dim and distant past. Conversely, the English poet speaks directly on the subject of the Roman poet's melancholy vision.

FURTHER READING
W.Y. Sellar, *The Roman Poets of the Augustan Age: Virgil,* Clarendon Press, Oxford, 1877
    Virgil as he was presented to the Victorians; still a sound introduction

R.H. Super, ed., *Matthew Arnold: On the Classical Tradition*, University of Michigan Press, 1960
    Includes the essay 'On the Modern Element in Literature'

Norman Vance, 'Virgil and the Nineteenth Century' in *Virgil and his Influence: Bimillenial Studies*, edited by Charles Martindale, Bristol Classical Press, 1984

THE MODERN ERA

In the modern era, Virgil's supremacy has been newly challenged. The American poet and critic Ezra Pound (1885–1972), one of the founding fathers of 'modernism', in a letter of 1916 (*The Letters of Ezra Pound 1907–1941*, edited by D.D. Paige, Faber, 1951, p. 138) called Virgil 'a second-rater, a Tennysonianised version of Homer' which was not a compliment to either Tennyson or Virgil. With hindsight this might be seen to some extent as a reaction on the part of a leading champion of the modernist movement against what might be regarded as two poetic pillars of the literary establishment. The English poet Robert Graves (1895–1985) had a similar lifelong antipathy to Virgil. In his *Oxford Addresses on Poetry* (Cassell, 1962), he provocatively presents Virgil as an 'Anti-Poet', a rule-ridden mechanical versifier without any originality or true poetic inspiration at all. 'Virgil's pliability; his subservience; his narrowness; his denial of that stubborn imaginative freedom that the true poets who preceded him had valued; his perfect lack of originality, courage, humour, or even animal spirits – these were the negative qualities which first commended him to government circles, and have kept him in public favour ever since.' In the analysis that follows, he shows a modern poet's lack of sympathy for the traditional devices of poetic **rhetoric** too. It is clear that he associated Virgil with all that in the wake of his experience in the First World War, he wished to turn his back on in the British literary and educational establishment of the interwar years.

As a result of the researches of Milman Parry in the 1930s into the oral character of the Homeric poems, the distinction between oral or primary epic on the one hand (Homer) and literary or secondary epic on the other (Virgil) were more sharply perceived than ever. In his witty poem 'Secondary Epic', W.H. Auden (1907–73) provides an **ironic** comment on the imperial theme of the *Aeneid*:

No, Virgil, no:
Not even the first of Romans can learn
His Roman history in the future tense,
Not even to serve your political turn;
Hindsight as foresight makes no sense.

This poem was published in 1960 but it echoes an earlier wariness about traditional attitudes regarding the politics of the *Aeneid* (and about Virgil's motives). It also reflects the disillusionment of a generation that had either experienced directly or grown up in the wake of the radical change of consciousness brought about by the First World War. Yet even though Auden's poem mocks its politics and repeats the notion that in writing it Virgil prostituted his muse, the continuing spell of his style is acknowledged in a beautifully well-crafted couplet:

Behind your verse so masterfully made
We hear the weeping of a Muse betrayed.

Yet for some readers events in the twentieth century have brought Virgil nearer. There is much anecdotal evidence about young men from English public schools (presumably with heroic dreams) going to war in 1914 with copies of Homer in their pockets. The experience of modern trench warfare changed attitudes in a way that made Homer seem much more remote from the modern world and Virgil nearer to modern sensibilities. That Virgil came from a civilisation that was more mature than Homer's was one of the arguments of T.S. Eliot in his foundation address to the Virgil Society in 1944, 'What is a Classic?' He cites as an example of such maturity the encounter of Aeneas with Dido in Hades: that Aeneas is unable to forgive himself for the hurt inflicted on Dido testifies to 'civilised consciousness and conscience'. This essay together with his earlier 'Virgil and the Christian world' from the leading exponent of modernism provided a counterweight to the denigration of the Roman poet by some leading practitioners of the twentieth century. So too did Herman Broch's novel *The Death of Virgil,* written in Germany on the brink of the Second World War, which presented a sympathetic picture of the poet on his deathbed in an agony of doubt about the role of art in the state, indeed doubting the very validity of art and wondering whether to consign the *Aeneid* to the flames (see Background, on Virgil's Life & Works).

Much modern academic criticism may be roughly divided into two schools. There are studies which sharing Eliot's line have seen the *Aeneid* not as a weak and artificial imitation of Homeric epic but as a creative reinvention of the form in which the mature values of civilisation, all that may be represented in *pietas*, triumph over the unreason, madness and chaos that is represented by the image of *furor impius*, which Jupiter prophecies will be bound in chains in the temple of Janus (Book 1, line 294). Juno's anger is finally contained and she is reconciled to the new dispensation (Book 12, lines 808–42). The poem envisions a stable order of beneficent empire. This optimistic school of interpretation, largely European, is countered by a more pessimistic view, largely American and sometimes called the Harvard school (from the origin of its leading proponents). For this school of interpretation, the triumph is largely an illusion; the present action of the poem exists in a twilight world replete with insubstantial encounters in which the promise of fulfilment is never quite realised. Furthermore, the note of anger on which the poem ends represents the triumph of Juno and all that she embodies.

In the last two decades, the study of literature has been increasingly influenced by new waves of theoretical criticism emanating from continental Europe and the United States. So far this has not made the kind of impact upon classical studies that is apparent in the study of English texts. However, the prevailing vogue for post-colonial studies and feminist approaches has resulted in new perspectives upon the poem in ways that will be apparent from Critical Approaches in this Note. Given the historical reality centring upon issues of conquest, dispossession, colonisation and resistance, it is possible to view the *Aeneid* from a non-Roman point of view and the general patriarchal design easily lends itself to a feminist critique. But probably the most interesting of the new theoretical perspectives for consideration in relation to the *Aeneid* arises from **reception theory**. This is a branch of **reader-response criticism** and involves a rejection of the assumptions of the **New Criticism** about the autonomy of the text and of traditional historical criticism about the fixity of meaning and the objectivity of evaluation. Critics embracing reader-response theory see the meaning of a text as 'created' or 'produced' by readers, and therefore as an unstable entity.

Reception theory considers readers and texts in relation to the perspective
of time, arguing that readers bring to the text the 'aesthetic horizon' of
their own time – a collection of expectations, prejudices and tolerances,
that is constantly shifting and evolving, not least because it encompasses
and absorbs into itself the tradition of interpretations that build up in
relation to a particular text, and become part of its meaning. There is no
fixed meaning in texts, but only that which is produced by the 'dialogue'
between the horizons of different generations. Clearly the *Aeneid* is
virtually a unique text by which to test such a theory as there are so many
reader responses through different ages to the text because of the unique
position occupied by the poem in the history of the Western tradition.
Ancient texts have necessarily had more generations of readers than
anything written in the vernacular. Greek texts are older than the Roman
but because of the dominance of Latin in European education until quite
recently they have never been read as widely. Given Virgil's primacy as a
model of elegant Latinity in verse, there has been a greater variety of
attention given to the *Aeneid*, the chief of his works, than to any other
classical text through the ages. Furthermore, since the poem has an
explicit historical and political dimension in its connection with Roman
origins and the **Augustan** present, there is an evident interaction with the
politics and history of different readers with widely divergent political
perspectives in various phases of the Western tradition. Reception theory
also raises issues that have to do with translation: if there is no
unmediated access to a fixed primary meaning, what is the status of
translation? What can be reasonably expected of translation, and what
should a translator aim for? Such questions have been debated and will
continue to be debated in relation to Virgil, particularly in view of the
disappearance of Latin and the consequent need for further translation.

FURTHER READING

C.M. Bowra, *From Virgil to Milton*, Macmillan, 1945

> One of the first modern accounts that sees Virgil not as the culmination of the
> ancient epic tradition but as the fountainhead of all subsequent epic development

Herman Broch, *The Death of Virgil*, translated by Jean Starr
Untermeyer, Routledge & Kegan Paul, 1946, reprinted 1977

> A major modern novel that has stimulated much interest in Virgil

Colin Burrow, 'Virgil in English translation', in *The Cambridge Companion to Virgil*, edited by Charles Martindale, Cambridge University Press, 1993

A lively overview of all the translations in English

Colin Burrow, *Epic Romance: Homer to Milton*, Oxford University Press, 1993

A study of the interplay between traditional epic and medieval romance

T.S. Eliot, *On Poetry and Poets*, Faber & Faber, London, 1956

Contains 'What is a Classic?' (1944) and 'Virgil and the Christian World (1951)

K.W. Gransden (ed.), *Virgil in English*, Penguin Books, 1996

An excellent selection from all the translations beginning with Chaucer

R. Heinze, *Vergil's Epic Technique*, translated by H. and D. Harvey & F. Robertson, Bristol Classical Press, 1993

The German original of 1915 was one of the first modern studies to answer the adverse criticism of German Romanticists who viewed Virgil as a second-rate Homer

W.F. Jackson Knight, *Roman Vergil*, Faber & Faber, 1944

A study that incorporates the insights of anthropology and psychology

W.R. Johnson, *Darkness Visible: A Study of Virgil's Aeneid*, University of California Press, 1976

Inclines to the 'pessimistic' school noted above

Charles Martindale, ed., *The Cambridge Companion to Virgil*, Cambridge University Press, 1997

The three sections (Translation and reception, Genre and poetic career, Contexts of production) include a variety of approaches from traditional scholarship to modern theory. It is well indexed and the list of works cited constitutes a generous bibliography. Illuminates usefully any Virgilian topic

Charles Martindale, *Redeeming the Text: Latin Poetry and the hermeneutics of reception*, Cambridge University Press, 1993

Virgil is discussed in relation to Dante and Lucan in the light of modern theory

Brookes Otis, *Virgil: A Study in Civilised Poetry*, Oxford University Press, 1964

Of the 'optimistic' school noted above, emphasising the triumph of *pietas* over *furor*

THE MODERN ERA continued

Adam Parry, 'The two voices of Virgil's *Aeneid*, in *Virgil: A Collection of Critical Essays*, edited by S. Commager, Prentice Hall, 1966
> The two voices are the public and the private: of the 'pessimistic' school noted above

V. Poschl, *The Art of Virgil: Image and Symbol in the Aeneid* [1950], translated by G. Seligson, University of Michigan Press, 1962
> Of the 'optimistic' school noted above

Gareth Reeves, *T.S. Eliot: A Virgilian Poet*, Macmillan, 1989
> A full length study of a leading twentieth-century Virgilian

M.R. Scherer, *The Legends of Troy in Art and Literature*, Phaidon Press,1963
> Contains a chapter dedicated to the *Aeneid*

R.D. Williams, & T.S. Pattie, eds, *Virgil: His Poetry Through the Ages*, The British Library, 1982
> Produced to accompany a bimillennial exhibition at the British Library

Theodore Ziolkowski, V*irgil and the Moderns*, Princeton University Press. 1993
> A wide-ranging comparative survey of Virgil in European literature (including French, German and Italian) with particular emphasis on the interwar years

BIBLIOGRAPHY

THE LATIN TEXT

H. Rushton Fairclough, *Virgil with an English Translation*, 2 vols., revised edition, Loeb classical Library, Heinemann 1935 and subsequently reprinted many times
> The Latin text with a prose translation on the facing page

R.D. Williams (ed.), *The Aeneid of Virgil*, with introduction and notes, Books 1–6, Macmillan, 1972, Books 7–12, 1973
> With notes intended to be helpful to beginners

Standard works of reference

Sir John E. Sandys, ed., *A Companion to Latin Studies,* 3rd edition, Cambridge University Press, 1935; reprinted by Hafner Publishing, 1963

Simon Hornblower & Antony Spawforth, eds, *The Oxford Classical Dictionary: The Ultimate Reference Work on the Classical World,* 3rd edition, Oxford University Press, 1996

John Boardman, Jasper Griffin & Oswyn Murray, eds, *The Oxford History of the Classical World,* Oxford University Press, 1986

H.H. Scullard, *From the Gracchi to Nero: A History of Rome from 133 BC to AD 68,* 2nd edition, Methuen, 1963

Michael Grant & John Hazel, eds, *Who's Who in the Classical Mythology,* Weidenfield & Nicolson, 1979

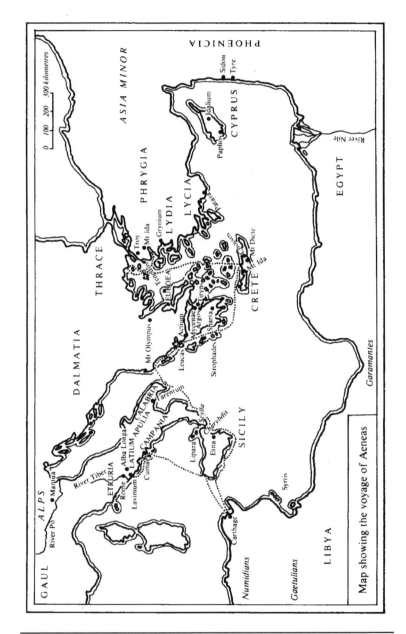

Map showing the voyage of Aeneas

CHRONOLOGY

BC	Historical events	Literary world
1250(c)	Destruction of Troy	
1000(c)	Latins settle in Latium	
815(c)	Foundation of Carthage from Tyre	
776	The first Olympiad	
750(c)		Possible date for creation of Greek Homeric poems, the *Odyssey* and the *Iliad*
625(c)	Founding of Rome	
610-580		Greek poet Sappho is born and dies
535(c)		Evidence that Homeric poems were put in order to be recited at Athenian festival; Thespis and the beginnings of Greek tragedy at Athens
509	Foundation of the Roman Republic after expulsion of Tarquin kings	
508	Athenians reform constitution, paving way to democracy	
496	Romans defeat Latins at Lake Regillus	
490	Greeks defeat Persian invasion at Marathon	Classical period begins
458		Aeschylus, the *Oresteia*
432		Sophocles, *Oedipus the King*
431	Worship of Apollo introduced at Rome; completion of Parthenon at Athens	
405		Euripedes, *The Bacchae*
399		Death of Socrates

BC	Historical events	Literary world
390	Rome invaded by Gauls	
385		Plato's *Republic*
340(c)		Aristotle's *Poetics*
322	Alexander of Macedon completes conquest of mainland Greece; end of democracy in Athens	
264-241	First Punic War between Romans and Carthaginians	
240(c)		Livius Andronicus, a freed Greek slave, translates *Odyssey* into Latin; first Roman poem, *Punic War,* by Gnaeus Naevius
218-202	Second Punic War; Hannibal invades Italy	
201	Worship of Cybele introduced in Rome	
180		Aristarchus heads Alexandrian library – Homeric poems edited
180(c)		Ennius, *Annales*
161		Marcus Porcus Cato banishes all Greek philosophers and rhetoricians from Rome (temporary)
145	Destruction of Rome	
100	Caius Julius Caesar born	
86(c)		Poet Catullus born
82-78	Dictatorship of Sulla	
75	Pirates capture Caesar on way to Rhodes; after paying ransom he has them crucified	
70		**Publius Vergilius Maro (Virgil)** born near Cremona in Transpadane region of Italy

BC	Historical events	Literary world
68	Augustus Octavianus Caesar born	
65		Horace, poet and author of *Ars Poetica,* born
60	First Triumvirate is secretly formed to rule Roman Empire; Caesar joins forces with Crassus and Pompey	
59	Caesar elected consul	
58-51	Gaul subjugated by Caesar; of 3 million population, 1 million killed, 1 million enslaved; in 55 and 54 invades Britain	
53	Crassus, now governor in Syria, killed by Parthians	
52	Pompey elected 'Consul without colleagues'; Senate demands that Caesar disband his armies	
50		Livy, writer, born at Padua
49	Julius Caesar grants full citizenship to the Transpadani	
49-46	Caesar declares war on Pompey and Senate by crossing Rubicon and invading Italy from Gaul; three years of civil war	
48	Pompey defeated at Pharsalus, flees to Egypt and is murdered; Caesar becomes Cleopatra's lover	
46	Victory at Thapsus leaves Caesar undisputed dictator of Rome	
44	Julius Caesar murdered in Republican conspiracy headed by Brutus and Cassius; Caesar's grand-nephew Octavian becomes consul	
43	New second triumvirate formed by Antony, Lepidus and Caesar's Octavian	
43(c)		Roman poet Ovid born; Cicero dies

BC	Historical events	Literary world
42	Antony defeats Cassius and then Brutus at Philippi; Julius Caesar declared a god	Horace, disillusioned with Brutus, abandons military career, and goes to Rome to write poetry
41		After dispute with soldier over land Virgil and father move to Rome
40	Antony controls East (where he forms liaison with Cleopatra); Lepidus Africa, and Octavian the West	Catullus dies
37		Virgil writes the *Eclogues*
32-30	Octavian turns popular opinion against Antony and Cleopatra	
31	Battle of Actium, Octavian's naval victory over Antony and Cleopatra; Octavian unchallenged champion of Roman world	
30	Egypt becomes Roman province	
29		Virgil publishes the *Georgics* and begins writing his epic *Aeneid*
27	Octavian becomes Emperor Augustus, Rome's first emperor for 400 years; his shrewd reforms lead to 250 years of stability in Roman Empire	
23	Death of Marcellus, Augustus's heir	
19		Virgil dies with *Aeneid* unfinished

allegory in Greek means saying one thing in terms of another and is used rather loosely in connection with Virgil

alliteration a sequence of repeated consonantal sounds in a stretch of language

apostrophe a rhetorical term for a speech addressed to a person, idea or thing, often placed at the start of a poem or essay, but also acting as a pause or digression in an ongoing statement

assonance the correspondence, or near-correspondence, in two words of the stressed vowel and sometimes those which follow

Augustan derived from the name of Rome's first emperor who ruled from 27BC to AD14, a time of peace and prosperity in which the leading poets Virgil and Horace were patronised by the regime to which they gave their support. Sometimes used to denote qualities of urbanity, poise, refinement and restraint embodied in Roman poets and aspired to by English poets

decasyllabic a line of verse of ten syllables

divine machinery a collective noun for the gods and goddesses, so called from their use as plot devices or mechanisms. Juno's anger sets the plot in motion and is instrumental in motivating the opposition to the Trojan/Roman destiny which is supported by Jupiter

epic a work of art (usually a poem) on a grand scale, written in a grand style with heroic figures involved in a great enterprise. The *Aeneid* is a defining type of the genre with a unified plot diversified by numerous episodes, and such features as divine machinery, set speeches, formal epithets, and extended similes. As a written poem the *Aeneid* has been contrasted to the Homeric epics which were composed and recited orally; it has been called literary or secondary in contrast to the oral or primary epic of Homer

episode a part of the poem that is self-contained and not strictly necessary for the main plot, e.g., the games in Book 5

epithet the Greek word for adjective (derived from the Latin), used of the regular adjectives describing persons, places and things, e.g., 'pious' Aeneas, 'trusty' Achates

figurative language, figures of speech (Latin, to shape, form or conceive) any form of expression or grammar which deviates from the plainest expression of meaning is designated a 'figure of speech'. These may be figures which alter the sense (*tropes*) like metaphor, or figures of arrangement which by their patterning give emphasis and memorability

genre a literary type or kind such as pastoral, georgic, epic or detective fiction with its own conventions and characteristics. These are never fixed; if they were, change and development would be impossible; Virgil renews and adapts the conventions of epic as exemplified in Homer

georgic (Greek, 'worker on the land', 'farmer') a genre that treated agricultural matters. Virgil's *Georgics* comprise a poem in four books treating crops, trees, animals and bees

hexameter from the Greek word for six (*hex*) and the word for measure (*metron*); the metre of Virgil and Homer and later epic poets of antiquity

humanist a scholar of the 'humanities', that is, classical literature, history and philosophy; in the Renaissance, reason, balance and a proper dignity for man were the central ideals of humanist thought based upon the revival of ancient ideals of human life and living

hyperbole (Greek, 'throwing too far') a figure of speech that emphasises by exaggeration

irony saying one thing that has another meaning or implication

metaphor (Greek, 'carrying over') a metaphor goes further than a comparison between two different things or ideas by fusing them together; one thing is described as being another thing, thus 'carrying over' all its associations

neoclassical (Greek 'new' and Latin 'classic') an adjective used to denote in the seventeenth and eighteenth century any literature and art that sought to conform to the rules or models of Greek or Latin antiquity. English literature of the period from 1660 to 1750 is particularly marked by this tendency

New Criticism a major critical movement that recommended that a poem must be studied as a poem and not as a piece of biographical or sociological evidence, or literary-historical material, or as a demonstration of a psychological theory of literature, or for any other reason. Close reading of texts became the only legitimate critical procedure seeing the work as a linguistic construct

pastoral (Latin, 'shepherd') poetry featuring shepherd-singers situated in an idyllic landscape with associations of the Golden Age, a mythical time of peace, innocence and plenty when nature was spontaneously fruitful without the need for agriculture. Virgil's first poems were ten pastorals or eclogues

pathos moments in a work that evoke strong feelings of pity and sorrow are said to have this quality

periphrasis an indirect manner of describing or speaking

reader-response criticism a critical approach that rejects any assumption about the autonomy of the text or fixity of meaning; meaning is 'created' or 'produced' by readers and therefore is an unstable or changeable entity

reception theory a branch of reader-response criticism which focuses on the changing history of the reaction to texts by readers

Renaissance (French, 'rebirth') a term associated with the revival of interest in antiquity beginning in Italy in the fourteenth century and spreading northwards thereafter; a period term covering the first wave of European culture and applied principally to the fifteenth and sixteenth centuries

rhetoric (Greek, 'art of speaking) the art of speaking and writing effectively so as to persuade an audience, often with the use of figurative language: 'The figures of rhetoric'; Virgil has been regarded as an exemplary rhetorical poet

Romantic a period term used for the literature and art produced in the wake of the French revolution of 1789 until roughly 1830; the literature of this period consciously turned its back upon the ideals and practices of neoclassical poets

simile a comparison or likeness, often extended in Virgil and a chief source of poetic imagery

symbol something that represents or stands for, or is thought to typify something else by association, particularly a material thing representing an abstract idea

unity of action a series of actions linked by a probable or necessary chain of cause and effect

Robin Sowerby was educated at St Catharine's College, Cambridge, where he read Classics and English. He now lectures in the Department of English Studies at Stirling University. He is also the author of Advanced York Notes on Homer's *Iliad* and *Odyssey*, Shakespeare's *Antony and Cleopatra* and *As You Like It* and Pope's *The Rape of the Lock and Other Poems*. He has edited selections from Dryden and Pope and is the author of *The Classical Legacy in Renaissance Poetry*, Longman, 1994 and *The Greeks: An Introduction to their Culture*, Routledge, 1995.